THE MYSTICAL FOUNDATIONS

Of

FRANCIS BACON'S SCIENCE

DANIEL BRANCO

Translated by Samuel Henriques de Araújo

The Mystical Foundations of Francis Bacon's Science
Daniel Branco
Translated by Samuel Henriques de Araújo

© Manticore Press, Melbourne, Australia, 2020.

All rights reserved, no section of this book may be utilized without permission, except brief quotations, including electronic reproductions without the permission of the copyright holders and publisher. Published in Australia.

Thema Classification:
PDA (Philosophy of Science), PDX (History of Science), QRM3 (Religion & Science), QRVK2 (Mysticism), VXW (Occult Interests), QRAB (Philosophy of Religion).

978-0-6487660-0-1

MANTICORE PRESS
WWW.MANTICORE.PRESS

ACKNOWLEDGMENTS

I'd like to thank *The Francis Bacon Society*, who funded the translation of this book into English, and Mr. Samuel Henriques de Araújo, who provided the translation. My family, friends, and everyone who believes in this work are grateful to you! Thank you!

LIST OF TABLES & IMAGES

Figure 1: The Rose Cross Temple, Theophilus Schweighardt Constantiens   40

Table 1: A Comparison of Protestant Doctrines and the Science of Bacon   102

CONTENTS

1. GENERAL INTRODUCTION — 7

2. THE INFLUENCE OF MYSTICISM ON BACON'S THOUGHT — 13
   - 2.1 Preliminary Questions — 13
   - 2.2 Mysticism and Cosmology in Bacon — 26
   - 2.2.1 *Pan, Cupid, Magic, and Gravitation* — 29
   - 2.3 Bacon and the Mystery Schools — 32
   - 2.4 Mysticism in *New Atlantis* — 34
   - 2.5 Hermeticism, Neoplatonism, and Monism in Bacon — 42
   - 2.5.1 *Rhetoric, Conspiracy, and Magic* — 49
   - 2.6 Baconian Mysticism and Aristotle: Asymmetries & Possible Confluences — 51
   - 2.6.1 *Baconian Mysticism: Aristotelian Metaphysics & Epistemology* — 52
   - 2.6.2 *Baconian Mysticism: Aristotelian Physics & Ethics* — 59

3. THE INFLUENCE OF PROTESTANT CHRISTIANITY ON BACON'S THOUGHTS — 67
   - 3.1 Preliminary Questions — 68
   - 3.2 Bacon and Puritanism: Similarities and Differences — 74
   - 3.3 Epistemology, Divine Philosophy, and Method — 81
   - 3.4 The Theologization of Science — 89
   - 3.4.1 *The Creation of the World in Six Days* — 94
   - 3.5 Bacon, Eschatology, and Roman Catholicism — 98
   - 3.6 Comparative Table Describing the Influence of Religion on Bacon — 102
   - 3.7 The Influence of These Ideas on Bacon's Criticism of the Ancients — 103
   - 3.7.1 *Transcendence and Immanence: Criticism and Concession* — 103
   - 3.7.2 *Responses to Platonic Dualism and to the Realistic Interpretation of Aristotelian Philosophy* — 106
   - 3.7.3 *Aristotle and Democritus* — 111
   - 3.7.4 *Bacon: Neither Opposed to Plato nor Contrary to Aristotle* — 113

4. THE INDUCTIVE METHOD OF BACON: ITS STRUCTURE AND COMPLEXITY — 115
   - 4.1 The Inductive Method Itself: Introductory Questions — 116
   - 4.2 The Question of the Functionality of Method: Tables of Presence, Absence, and Comparison — 117
   - 4.2.1 *The Forms and Law of the Act* — 120
   - 4.2.2 *The Problem of Intermediaries and Realism* — 123
   - 4.3 What is Baconian Epistemology? Some Possibilities — 126

4.4 A Techné	129
4.5 Induction and Ethics	132
4.6 Scientific Neutrality	134
4.7 The Royal Society, Science, and Politics	135
4.8 Bacon, General Systems Theory, and Epistemology of Systems Thinking	138
4.9 Summary of Sections 1-8	144
4.10 The Real Causes of Bacon's Critique of the Ancients and Aristotle	145
5. BACON AGAINST THE MISINTERPRETATIONS OF HIS LEGACY	**149**
5.1 Bacon and Modernity	149
5.2 Bacon and the Contemporary World	159
5.3 Concessions and Critical Appraisal	166
6. CONCLUSION	**169**
References	173

1.

GENERAL INTRODUCTION

Up to now, the academic work on Francis Bacon in Brazil has focused on his legacy as a scientist, founder of the inductive method, and "father of modern science." The aim of this work is different to these publications. It sets out to investigate another aspect of this controversial and well known author, that of the mystical. We will study the science of Bacon, while considering the influence of mysticism on him. Thus, the intention is to present a substantial contribution to the understanding of the author with an interpretation of his work that differs from those currently in circulation. For this, different works by the author will be used, among which are *Novum Organum, The Advancement of Learning, New Atlantis, The Wisdom of the Ancients,* and *Essays on Morality and Politics*. The concept of "mystical" here may include 1) religiosity, 2) spiritualism, 3) esoteric thinking of mystery schools, and 4) philosophical concepts of the Eastern world. At times, in order to provide clarity, however, "mystic" will be used specifically for points 3 and 4, whilst points 1 and 2 will be considered under the influence of the Christian religion on Bacon. Thus, the intention is to facilitate an understanding of the author with an interpretation of his work that is different from the usual perspective.

We will also study the Baconian inductive method in order to make it clear in the last chapter that the relation between Bacon and contemporary science must be studied on the basis of the total picture of Baconian thought, which includes both the idea of the inductive method and the influence of mysticism.

The first chapter, entitled *The Influence of Mysticism on Bacon's Thought*, will introduce the mystical influences on Bacon. The section *Preliminary Questions* will provide a historical description of Hermeticism and mysticism. *Mysticism and Cosmology in Bacon* will specify that mystical presence in the author's cosmology. The subsection *Pan, Cupid, Magic, and Gravitation* will study the considerations of Bacon on the myths of Pan and Cupid as a source of knowledge for cosmology. The next section, *Bacon and the Mystery Schools*, will investigate the relationship between Bacon and the esotericism of the mystery schools, specifically the Rosicrucian. The section *Mysticism in New Atlantis* will describe the mystical elements present in the New Atlantis symbolism. The following section, *Hermeticism, Neoplatonism, and Monism in Bacon*, will make an investigation of the presence of Hermetic ideas, Neoplatonists, and monists in his thought. The subsection *Rhetoric, Conspiracy, and Magic* will address the premise that, although it was still considered conspiracy, there was support for the idea that Bacon was the true author of Shakespeare's work and that he used poetic rhetoric in these works to disseminate his esoteric ideas. Starting from the section *Baconian Mysticism and Aristotle: Asymmetries & Possible Confluences* we will investigate points in the thoughts of Bacon and Aristotle – it is worth noting that Plato will sometimes be mentioned also, due to the importance of his philosophy for the understanding of Aristotle. The first subsection is *Baconian Mysticism: Aristotelian Metaphysics & Epistemology*, which will discuss the confluences and asymmetries in the concept of metaphysics and epistemology. *Baconian Mysticism: Aristotelian Physics & Ethics* will occupy the next subsection, dealing with the agreements and disagreements between both in the field of physics and ethics respectively.

The second chapter entitled *The Influence of Protestant Christianity on Bacon's Thoughts* will study the influence of religion—especially Anglican and Puritan Christianity—on Bacon. Here Bacon's religiosity will be synonymous with "mysticism." The first section, *Preliminary Questions*, will contextualize historically the religiosity that surrounded Bacon's life. The second section, *Bacon and Puritanism: Similarities and Differences*, will study Bacon's relationship with the Puritan movement. The third section,

Epistemology, Divine Philosophy, and Method, will investigate the relationship between the Baconian concepts of epistemology and Divine Philosophy with its inductive method. *The Theologization of Science*, which constitutes the fourth section, discusses the theological concepts that Bacon applies to his science. The subsection entitled *The Creation of the World in Six Days* provides the mystical interpretation that Bacon offers on the biblical account of the creation of the world in six days. In the fifth section, *Bacon, Eschatology, & Roman Catholicism* we specifically investigate Bacon's application of the religious concept of eschatology in his science. This section also deals with Bacon's criticism of Roman Catholicism, and more specifically scholasticism. The next section provides a comparative picture and describes the influence of religion on Bacon. The final section, entitled *The Influence of These Ideas on Bacon's Critique of the Ancients* studies the influence of these ideas on Bacon's critical discourse on ancient thinkers. This section is divided into four subsections. The first, *Transcendence and Immanence: Criticism and Concession*, explains both the similarities and the dissimilarities between Bacon and the ancients taking into consideration the Baconian concepts of transcendence and immanence. The second section, *Responses to Platonic Dualism and to the Realistic Interpretation of Aristotelian Philosophy*, studies the possible impact of a new reading of Plato and Aristotle, and, more precisely, the extent of rejection or the acceptance of these philosophers by Bacon. *Aristotle and Democritus*, the third subsection, discusses the influence of Democritus on Bacon, as well as the impact of this influence on his criticism of Aristotle. The final subsection, *Bacon: Neither Opposed to Plato nor Contrary to Aristotle*, explains how the legacy of Plato and Aristotle was not entirely denied by Bacon.

The fourth chapter, entitled *The Inductive Method of Bacon: Its Structure and Complexity* studies the Baconian inductive method itself. In addition to the relevance of presenting Bacon's inductive method, this chapter will connect the first two chapters to the fourth and final chapter in which Bacon's mystique and method will negotiate with the modern and contemporary sciences. The first section, *The Inductive Method Itself: Introductory Questions*, will introduce the method. The next section, *The Question of the Functionality of Method: Tables of Presence, Absence, and Comparison*, will discuss Baconian ideas about the Presence, Absence, and Comparison tables, clarifying practical aspects of the method. This section will be divided into two subsections. The first, *The Forms and Law of the Act*, will investigate the Baconian concept of form and the idea he had designated as the Law of the Act. The second, *The Problem of Intermediates and Realism*, will discuss the Baconian concept of intermediaries in induction and its implementation in their method, considering Bacon's theory of knowledge and the idea that he may or may not have been a naive realist. The third section, *What is Baconian Epistemology? Some Possibilities* follows the previous subsection, banishing the notion that Bacon was a naive realist, and explores viable possibilities for the development of a substantial thesis on what the Baconian epistemology is. *A Techné*, the next section, examines the concept of technique in Bacon and its use in the inductive method. The fifth section, *Induction and Ethics*, studies the relationship between the Baconian inductive method and ethics. The sixth section, *Scientific Neutrality*, discusses the concept of neutrality in Bacon's method and thinking. The seventh section, *The Royal Society, Science, and Politics*, explains Bacon's influence on the scientific academy—more precisely on the *Royal Society*—and investigates Bacon's political and scientific ambitions. The eighth section, *Bacon, General Systems Theory and Epistemology of Systems Thinking*, studies the similarities and dissimilarities between Bacon's thought, General Systems Theory, and the Epistemology of Systems Thinking. The following section will summarize all previous sections. Finally, the tenth section, *The Real Causes of Bacon's Critique of the Ancients and Aristotle*, is based on the previous chapter on science and induction in Bacon, and discusses his criticisms of the ancients and Aristotle in greater depth.

The fourth and final chapter entitled *Bacon: Against the Misinterpretations of His Legacy*, uses the studies of Bacon's mysticism and science made in the first three chapters, to investigate the true dimension of Bacon's legacy and make a critical assessment of the acceptance of Bacon's thought by the academy. The first section, entitled *Bacon and Modernity*, studies the differences and similarities between Bacon and modernity. The second section, *Bacon and the Contemporary World*, investigates the similarities and dissimilarities between Bacon and contemporary thought. The third and final section, *Concessions and Critical Appraisal*, will make a final evaluation of the criticisms of Bacon and the enduring legacy of his mysticism, science, and thoughts.

2.

THE INFLUENCE OF MYSTICISM ON BACON'S THOUGHT

THIS CHAPTER EXPLAINS THE INFLUENCE OF HERMETIC and Neoplatonic mysticism on Bacon's ideas, especially his criticism of Aristotle's philosophy. In the first section, we introduce the Hermetic context. In the second section, we investigate the relationship between mysticism and Bacon's conception of the cosmos. In the later section, we study Bacon's relationship with the mystery schools, especially the Rosicrucian school. The fourth section will explain Baconian mysticism in *New Atlantis*. The fifth section will study the relationship between Hermeticism, Neoplatonism, monism, and Baconian thought. The sixth and final section will investigate the confluences and asymmetries between Baconian mysticism, Aristotelian metaphysics, epistemology, physics, and ethics. Although it contains comments on Aristotle's philosophy, this chapter is not intended to delve into Aristotelian thought, but rather to present it in general, since the subject of the chapter is Bacon's point of view.

2.1 *Preliminary Questions*

Gnosticism and Hermeticism are not the same thing. The first is dualistic. The second, if understood as a development of Plotinian Neoplatonism, tends to monism. There are cases where the so-called Gnostics have come close to monistic postulates—such as Valentianism and Setianism—and in which Gnosticism and

Hermeticism are considered synonymous. However, the dualistic influence of pre-Plotinian Platonism and Persian Manichaenism creates a point of separation between both systems. There is a form of gnosis in Hermeticism, but it should not be confused with the dualistic gnosis of the *Gnostikoi*. Gnostics referred to by Irenaeus of Lyons, Origen, Epiphanius of Salamanina, Clement of Alexandria, and Hippolytus of Rome—such as the Marcionists, the Naassenes, the Ophites, the Pricilians, and the Peratas, among others—had in common a dualistic view of the world.

Marcion opposed the Old Testament God to Jesus of the New Testament, teaching that there was no continuity between them and that the creator of the material world was not good as the Deliverer. The Naassenes taught that our primordial habitation (the Garden of Eden) represented the spiritual body – the Garden was the head, Paradise was the brain, the Pisom River was the eyes, the River Giom was the vision, the River Tigre was breath and smell, and the River Euphrates was the mouth. The Ophites believed that Jesus did not have a material body and that it was incorruptible light, called the creator of Ialdabaoth (translated as Son of Chaos), which said that Adam and Eve gained a "carnal" body only after the Fall, providing Mother Sophia with a crucial function in the redemption process of men. The Peratas illustrated their cosmology by claiming the body-matter, like the Hebrew people, sought liberation. The Pricilians practiced abstinence from sex, wine, and meat. They also taught the existence of two kingdoms: one of light, incorporeal and symbolized by the twelve patriarchs, and another of darkness and material form symbolized by the twelve signs of the zodiac.

Manichaean dualism deepened the dualism between good and evil already existing in the Zoroastrian religion of Persia – in the case of Zoroastrianism Ahura Mazda was the god-being of good, and Ahriman was the god-being of evil. Manichaens said that there are three creations and in the third the "lower" is the human material body and in the first is the "light" (the Mandeans, another dualistic group, taught the superiority of an immaterial world over matter. They had a ritual of rebirth to represent this doctrine).

It was the Paulicians who, in addition to making the Demiurge an evil spirit, rejected the Tanakh (the Old Testament). The Bogomils, who considered the material world to be the work of Satan (or the Cathars and Albigenses) rejected the consumption of meat (condemning it as "murder") and the Catholic doctrine of the sacraments, claiming that their material nature was not apt to retain the divine. The Cathars or Albigenses were fought by the Catholic Church in the episode that became known as the Albigensian Crusade.

With the exception of "libertine" Gnostics, who believed that the body should stick to excesses, as Carpocrates taught, most Gnostics were ascetic and religiously iconoclastic. They were fought and formed separate sects of official Christianity.[1] Hermeticism, on the other hand, was theoretically monistic.

Plotinus traced a difference between him and the Gnostics by the fact that they believed that matter was evil, and he, Plotinus, did not.[2] Hermeticists believed, as shown by Hermes, that everything above is below. The Gnostics had a strong connection with Judaism and Hellenism. Hermeticism made direct reference to Egypt. Not that all this was common to both, but the context was different, and the appropriation of ideas occurred in different ways. Many Hermeticists were priests or religious, although they were considered heterodox. Just as contemplation, geometry, and speculation were prioritized by the Gnostics, experimentation and alchemy received strong attention from Hermeticists. The Gnostics valued their separate structures from official Christian civilization; the Hermeticists caused more revolutionary "damage" to Christianity. The Gnostic "escape from the world" did not resonate well with Renaissance Hermeticism, which operated more in the world of European humanism.

---

[1] JONAS, Hans. *La Religion Gnostica. El mensaje del Dios Extraño y los comienzos del cristianismo*. Traducción de Menchu Gutiérrez. Madrid: Ediciones Siruela, 2003.

[2] The plot of 'Plotinus against the Gnostics' could also be called 'against those who say that the Demiurge of the cosmos and the cosmos are evil'. See J. R, Baracat. Plotinus – *Enneads I, II, & III*; Porfírio – *The Life of Plotinus*. Trad br. Junior Baracat. Ph.D. Thesis – Pro-Rectory of Research and Post-Graduation in Philosophy, UNICAMP, Campinas, 2006. p. 455.

Medieval Europe was founded on Greek philosophy, albeit Christianized by the influence of Plato (428 BC-348 BC) on St. Augustine (354-430) and the influence of Aristotle (384-312 BC) on St. Thomas Aquinas (1225-1274). The Renaissance saw the flourishing of Greco-Roman art, which had long since been superseded by Christian culture. The turnaround in this period was due to a mystic and the artistic consciousness, rather than the apology to reason or rational faith, as Christians wanted. Certainly, the Middle Ages did not fail to recognize the forerunners of what would become the experimental philosophy that would influence modernity.

Men like Robert Grosseteste (1168-1253) and Roger Bacon (1214-1294) emphasized the necessity of observing nature for the understanding not only of the outside world, but also of man himself. Roger Bacon, for example, was associated with the study of lenses and optics, contributing to the invention of glasses. However, it was the Renaissance period that built a bridge to the modern world. The figure of Leonardo da Vinci (1452-1519) is also emblematic when one wants to speak of both Renaissance experimentalism and humanism, taking knowledge far beyond what was previously achieved. Aside from Da Vinci's work as a scientist, mathematician, engineer, inventor, anatomist, architect, inventor, poet, and botanist, his art (sculpture, painting, and music) cannot be studied without taking into account the influence of effervescent mystic thought.

Erasmus of Rotterdam (1466-1536), a Dutch Augustinian monk, was a well-known humanist of the late Middle Ages and early modernity. The author of *Laus stultitiae* (1511), also entered into fierce debate with the Protestant reformer Martin Luther (1483-1546) over the doctrine of predestination and revealed how precious the idea of free humanity was to him, and how man's autonomy was necessary to make evident the superiority of humanism over the oppression of what he believed to be a fatalistic Christianity.

Leonardo Bruni (1370-1444), a humanist influenced by Aristotle, especially *Nicomachean Ethics*, sought to reshape present thoughts and emphasized the need for virtuous social praxis. For Bruni, happiness consists in virtuous action. There was no reason for him to switch action for asceticism, for that would be to leave fulfillment and completeness for emptiness and inaccuracy, and goodness for vain frugality.[3]

Poggio Bracciolini (1380-1459) also disseminated several classic Latin writings, which contributed to the renewal of such thoughts towards the end of the Middle Ages. Similar to Leonardo Bruni, Bracciolini valued action over contemplation. For him, one cannot find nobility far from action. The noble man was, therefore, the practical man. The humanist Leon Battista Alberti (1404-1472), in turn, studied philosophy, devoting himself to the study of mathematics, architecture, and the criticism of epicurean philosophy, which he called happiness to do nothing. For Alberti, as for Bruni and Bracciolini, happiness is associated with action, in relation to the world. The *homo faber*, who is virtuous, is, according to Alberti, the one who cares not only for himself but also for the common good. Virtue, in his view, resembles the Greek *areté*, for it must perfect the whole man, making him capable of acting for the benefit of community life.

Gianozzo Manetti (1396-1459), Mateus Palmieri (1406-1475), and Ermolao Barbaro (1453-1493), also continued to exalt human nature, although they had individual peculiarities. The first, who translated the works of Aristotle and the Psalms of the Bible, claimed man was superior to other creatures. The second sought to build a bridge between the active life and the contemplative life, without forgetting

---

[3] "For the great exponents of Italian Humanism (such as Leonardo Bruni [...] Lorenzo Valla) to read the great classics of the ancient world means to return to a higher civilization than the one in which they lived and which constitutes the unattainable model of all forms of human coexistence. The humanists, however, were not passive repeaters, for in their writings a constant controversy was present not only against the 'barbarism' of medieval Scholastics but also against the dangers of repetition and Classicism [...] The writings discovered by the humanists, in the course of their great work of searching and commenting, did not constitute themselves as mere documents. Those ancient works, upon which the humanists applied their refined philology, contain—for their eyes—not only knowledge, but are at the same time directly useful to science and its practice. The diffusion of editions made directly from the Greek originals, that is, of translations no longer based (as in the Middle Ages) on Arabic translations of Greek works, had decisive effects on the development of scientific knowledge." ROSSI, Paolo. *The Birth of Modern Science in Europe*. Trad. br. Antonio Angonese. Bauru-SP: EDUSC, 2001, pp. 89-90.

the importance of the wise man in the city. The third was a translator of Aristotle who endeavored to provide future generations with a translation that was faithful to the thought of the Greek philosopher, that is, without the possible misrepresentations of the Middle Ages. For him, study made men wise and virtuous. Still, Lorenzo Valla (1401-1457) objected to stoic and monastic asceticism, exalting pleasure (not to be understood purely as carnal) as necessary to human achievement. He also affirmed, as a philologist, that the "word" cannot be forgotten by men, for it is the consideration of this "word" that makes them wise. Phrased another way, the discovery of the true meaning of 'what is' can be interpreted as liberating. Investigating several manuscripts, Valla sought to prove a manuscript was false. Called the *Donation of Constantine*, it was used by the Catholic Church in the attempt to prove the historicity of its temporal power. For him, therefore, this search for the "word" (or the meaning of texts and affirmations) makes man apt to live virtuously.[4]

In this period, what was understood as science differed substantially from the concept of science that the world (especially the Western) has in modernity. There was, at this time, a less delineated boundary between magic and science.

In the Renaissance Nicholas of Cusa (1401-1464) denied the supremacy of reason, and by denying it, indirectly criticized mere deductive thinking. For him, the awareness of the limitation of man before the infinite was a sign of true wisdom, worthy of a great philosopher.[5] Tommaso Campanella (1568-1639), in turn, valued the complexion of an authentic science and defended Galileo Galilei

---

[4] "In Valla [...] who had represented [in] Apollo the divine pre-science and in Jupiter omnipotence, that substitution is manifested by concrete symbolic forms of the abstract expressions of thought which Cassirer considers essential for the typical Renaissance way of thinking." ROSSI, Paolo. *Francis Bacon: From Magic to Science*, p. 211.

[5] "Nicholas of Cusa already anticipated [...] the Newtonian mechanicism. More than that, Creation itself, as traditionally conceived, was called into question. His relativism [...] was certainly revolutionary. In the thought of Nicholas of Cusa, an experimental domain was already constituted [...] that expresses an autonomy of the human intellectual creation and a new theory of the knowledge." WOORTMANN, Klaas. *Religion and Science in the Renaissance*. Brasília: UNB, 1997, p. 36.

(1564-1642) when he was accused of heresy for proposing the existence of the movement of the Earth around the sun. In his most famous work, *City of the Sun* (1623), he uses the metaphors of the sun and the priesthood to propose reforms to medieval society.

The discovery of works attributed to Hermes Trismegistus (identified as the Egyptian god Thoth, the Greek god Hermes and the Roman god Mercury), Zoroaster, and Orpheus was a landmark for the Renaissance movement. The mystical-theological-philosophical thinking of these works influenced this school of thought to propose reforms for the Christian worldview then in force. For them, the writings attributed to Hermes and Zoroaster were as old as the Old Testament of the Bible, and Hermes was considered, for some, as important as Moses. It was necessary then, as they understood it, to initiate a rediscovery of this ancient wisdom, since this power could fill the void present in medieval thought, and bring to light the truth obscured by the limitations of scholastic philosophy.

The practice of alchemy, which contributed to the birth of chemistry, derived from this effervescence of magic, was one of the activities that the Renaissance held in high esteem. To know whether a particular being contained the being or whether the being was always outside the being, was to question whether or not an ontology is possible. The transformation of objects, and therefore the conception of the real, must be subjective or everything is what it is, and reality can be known objectively. All these philosophical questions were indirectly associated with the curiosity of the alchemists.

During the Renaissance, Marsilius Ficino (1433-1499), a Neoplatonist in Florence, translated the *Corpus Hermeticum*. This bastion of ancient magic and science was translated into Italian, in his home country, which was important for its rediscovery, rendering philosophy into a magical knowledge which, if not experimental, was alchemy for the Renaissance.[6]

---

[6] "Marcílio Ficino is an exemplary case. He was regarded by the Enlightenment as a Neoplatonic scholar, but it was only in the twentieth century that he was discovered to be also a Neoplatonic magician, with his theories of magic and talismans, adept in the imaginary 'Hermes Trimegistus'. Ficino was a physician, but practiced Orphic magic through musical enchantments and 'sympathies'. He

However, it was Giovanni Pico della Mirandola (1463-1494) who united Neoplatonism, Christian theology, and the Cabala, with the teachings of Ficino. Giordano Bruno (1548-1600) also was seized with a great yearning for radical epistemological reform and, it can be said, also a political one. Even though he was sentenced to death, he did not deny what he considered to be an advance for humanity, philosophical, and mystical under which he proposed the consciousness of unity between man and nature.[7]

The beginning of modern science did not take place in a purely revolutionary way. Rather, it used ideas that had been developed over the centuries. Europe, by then, was already filled with various arguments about reality. Like any other form of thought, modern science has been shaped by the influences of those who came before. The precursors of the Western concept of science can be found in ancient Greece. Men like Democritus, Epicurus (341-270 BC), Hippocrates (460-370 BC), and Galen (129-217) did not possess a stagnant curiosity and tried to investigate nature in-depth, even if hard work had to be done.

Hippocrates is considered the first man to separate medicine from religion. For him, it was not necessary for men to possess the understanding that the function of medicine was different from theology. They also had to discover that the true physician had his own insightful method of study. Black bile, yellow bile, blood, and phlegm, according to Hippocrates, mediated human "humor," as did the relationship between the states of cold, hot, dry, and humid and the four seasons. In other words, the precursor of scientific medicine said that the four humors should be balanced, otherwise, by way of example, phlegm could make man phlegmatic and amenable to catarrhal disease, blood could render a man sanguineous

---

was also a cleric and justified his practices as 'natural magic', not demonic." Ibid., p. 109.

[7] "If Giordano Bruno was a defender of Copernicus, his defense was inspired by Asclepius (who described ancient Egyptian methods to animate the images of his gods from the cosmic powers) and 'Hermes Trismegistus'. He was a defender of Copernicus as much as Ficino was, but it is quite possible that his defense of the Copernican system was anchored in the conviction that the Copernican Sun corresponded to Ficino's solar magic." Ibid., p. 110.

and susceptible to blood diseases, black bile could make a man melancholic and susceptible to diasthetic diseases, and yellow bile could make a man bilious and susceptible to bilious diseases.[8] With his opinion of medicine, Hippocrates also sought to separate medicine from philosophy, since, for him, philosophy studies the whole man, while medicine studies the human body only, in order to maintain health. However, in developing a systematization, even if it failed, medical practice demonstrated the attempt to present to the city another useful instrument for the well-being of citizens.

Galen, a Greek physician who lived under the rule of the Roman Empire, was a strong critic of the medicine of his day. He accused contemporary physicians of straying from the teaching of Hippocrates, of being flawed in logic, of casting aside the proper method of study, of laziness, corruption, and of being factious. Galen was acclaimed in the Middle Ages and the Renaissance as the highest authority of medicine, as Aristotle was with philosophy. Galen believed, like Plato, in the tripartition of the soul – namely the division of the soul into the heart, the liver, and with the rational component present in the brain. In addition, he had an interest in biology and zoology. He was, therefore, a man who regarded study as a tool not to arrive at endless speculations about an abstract world, but to know the structure of the human, his nature.[9]

Ptolemy was perhaps to medieval astronomy what Euclid was to geometry. He formulated ideas to explain a series of natural phenomena that were mysterious for his time. Among such ideas are the immobility of Earth, the change of fixed stars in the sky as a consequence of the rotation of the spheres present in them, and the circular nature of the Earth at the center of the universe.[10] With such

---

[8] See HIPPOCRATES. *Writings*. Trad. Ing. Francis Adams. Chicago: Encyclopedia Britannica, 1952.

[9] "In the writings of the Greek physician Galenus, [...] we find [...] a teleological conception, [...] an identification of God and nature, [an] emphasis on the divine art, techné. Because of this devout teleological conception, Galen, like Seneca, was regarded by Christians of the Middle Ages and Renaissance as having been basically Christian." HOOYKAAS, R. *The Religion and the Development of Modern Science*. Trad. br. Fernando Dídimo Viveira. Brasília: UNB, 1988, p. 24.

[10] See PTOLEMY. *The Almagest*. Trad. Ing. C. Taliaferro. Chicago: Encyclopedia

ideas, Ptolemy was genuinely concerned with the epistemological problems of his time and endeavored to solve them, benefiting future generations.

Democritus developed the idea that physical reality, *physis*, was made up of atoms, tiny, indivisible particles. For the Greek philosopher, matter occurs due to the collision of atoms. This phenomenon also gives weight to them. Unlike Democritus, Epicurus admits the essential nature of weight in atoms. Moreover, for him, the atoms, which are constantly falling because of the weight, have the ability to deviate. On the other hand, Epicurus agrees with Democritus on the fact that the collision between atoms—which, for Epicurus, had a more accidental character— makes matter a reality.[11]

The Latin philosopher Lucretius (99-55 BC), who attempted to synthesize the thought of Epicurus, admitted that atoms fall in empty space and that their ability to deviate and the consequent clashes between them are the source of matter. The Latin thinker, however, asserted that atoms had several shapes, pointed, round, smooth, for example, and that although the shapes of atoms had a limit, the quantification of associations between equal atoms would be outside the calculations. Therefore, each distinct material body would be an arrangement of atoms different from each other. In this sense, also, the intangible would generate the tangible. Lucretius goes on to say that colors, even though arising from the atoms, do not receive any color from them. It was the association between different atoms that would make color exist, not a particular atomic set.[12]

Britannica, 1952.

[11] "One of the most striking differences between the system of Democritus and that of Epicurus concerns the genesis of the Cosmos... This philosophy [of Epicurus], as we know, was synthesized two centuries after the death of Epicurus by Lucretius in *De rerum natura*, a work that will later aid the revival of atomism in the Renaissance". *The Experimental Philosophy in Eighteenth-Century England: Francis Bacon and Robert Boyle*, São Paulo: FAPESP, 2004, pp. 68-69. See also EPICURO. *Anthology of Texts*. Trad. br. Agostinho da Silva. São Paulo: Abril Cultural, 1980.

[12] LUCRETIUS. *From Nature*. Trad. br. Agostinho da Silva. Abril Cultural, 1980.

It was common for European people between the end of the rebirth and the beginning of modern science—having absorbed all this range of thoughts that preceded them—to practice physiognomics, believing that they could know a person through the examination of physiognomy, the practice of chiromancy (predicting the future by reading the lines of the hands), and astrology, which sought to know what would happen by observing the stars.[13]

These facts illustrate that belief in the complexity of nature and the superiority of the cosmos in relation to the terrestrial orbit ended up defining this historical period. Neoplatonism and Renaissance Hermeticism were also present in the heliocentric theory of Nicolaus Copernicus (1473-1543). The idea that the sun was the center of the universe, elevating it to a status of superiority in relation to the abode of man, also revealed the influence of Hermeticism in regard to veneration of the sun. In addition, Copernicus was an admirer of the *Corpus Hermeticum*.[14]

Moreover, astrology was not despised by him. Tycho Brache (1546-1601), a Dane who sought to synthesize Ptolemy (90-168) and Copernicus, also believed that there was a relationship between the celestial world and the terrestrial world.[15] Indeed, the popular idea in antiquity and the Middle Ages that the sun revolved around the earth and that it was motionless, postulated mainly by the Greek

---

[13] SCHLIESSER, Eric. *Sympathy: A History*. New York: Oxford University Press, 2015, p. 91.

[14] "The medieval church had banished magic and made it abominable (and was itself abhorred by the Reformation, due to its 'sacramental magic'). But Renaissance, erudite magic, which condemned the ignorant magic of the past, was often part of the philosophy of the age. Copernicus reveals this. His revolutionary hypothesis was built upon mathematical calculations, but in *De Revolutionibus Orbium Coelestium* he invokes 'Hermes Trismegistus' as an argument for his heliocentrism." WOORTMANN, Klaas. *Religion and Science in the Renaissance*, p. 110.

[15] "More than a naturalistic philosopher, Tycho was a patient and extremely careful observer. Certainly the greatest of the naked eye observers who had the history of astronomy. His first observations date back to 1563, when he was only sixteen, and continued such investigations throughout the course of his life reaching such precision that many historians of astronomy were deemed almost incredible." ROSSI, Paolo. *The Birth of Modern Science in Europe*, p. 129.

astronomer Ptolemy, was based not only on observations of nature but on religious principles. Because the Bible said in the Book of Joshua that God had stopped the sun for an hour, and the Book of Ecclesiastics that the Earth always remains in its place, by way of example, questioning the nature of the Universe was not just *avant-garde*, it was subversive. Copernicus, afraid to proceed with his revolutionary thesis, did not live to see the repercussions it caused. Several times he endured existential crises due to what his thesis represented to the world. He was afraid of the consequences that his research could cause to people's lives.

Lutheran theologian Andreas Osiander (1498-1552) attempted to mitigate the impact of Copernicus' thesis by seeking to promote an interpretation of his work that made Copernican heliocentrism a system whose validity was only instrumental, and that it served to improve certain meteorological predictions on Earth, but was not to be believed as a description of nature.[16] That attitude, however, though it seems retrograde in the twenty-first century, was progressive for its time since it was an attempt to preserve Christian dogmas and at the same time keep the church receptive to the contribution of science. The great Protestant leaders of continental Europe, such as Luther, Melanchthon (1497-1560), and Calvin (1509-1564) opposed Copernicanism. For them, heliocentrism was not compatible with the Bible, and so biblical truth should be upheld to the detriment of science. Johannes Kepler (1571-1630), who had studied to be a Protestant pastor, however, supported the Copernican system. His assent to Copernicus consequently caused critical thoughts in relation to institutional Christianity, which had fractions that waged war against each other (Catholics and Protestants). He continued to be a Christian, but he can hardly be considered an orthodox Christian.[17]

---

[16] Professor of the Faculty of Wittenberg Gerg Rheticus (1514-1574) was favorable to Copernicus. See SOBEL, Dava. *A Heaven More than Perfect: How Copernicus Revolutionized the Cosmos*. Trad. br. Ana Cláudia Ferrari. São Paulo: Companhia das Letras, 2015.

[17] "Kepler [...] of Neoplatonism drew the aesthetic satisfaction for the new model, which nourished his artistic spirit. But the main source of his enthusiasm was mystical-religious and focused on the new dignity given to the Sun [...] Kepler espoused a kind of "astronomical theory" of the Trinity according to which the

When the Catholic Church, similarly to prominent Protestant theologians, rejected the revitalization and complementation of Galileo's (1564-1642) Copernicanism, it argued that the Church had held for centuries a consensus on the veracity of the literal interpretation the Bible which spoke of the movement of the sun and of the immobility of the Earth, and that ancient researchers had attested to this in their research.[18] Galileo, however, besides complementing the research of Copernicus, also promoted the independence of scientific research in relation to religion. For him, it was necessary to see biblical concepts as theological and spiritual truths that concerned the salvation of the souls of men. Science, however, should deal with the Book of Nature, material reality, and empirical observation. By doing so, a scientist would thus not be censured if his discovery contradicted any truth present in the Holy Scriptures.[19] The retraction by Galileo shows not only that he feared death, but still had respect for the authority of the Church.[20] This is evident when, on his deathbed, he surrendered his soul to God, hoping to find Eternal Life. Even though his goal was to separate science from religion, he did not seek to make science into an anti-religious institution. He ultimately wanted to reconcile the two. His reformation did not seek to destroy the religious legacy, but only to improve it. Instead of rupture, he wanted progress.[21]

Sun is the God Father; the sphere of the fixed stars is the God the Son, and the ether, the intervening instrument through which the power by which the sun drives the planets is transmitted, is the Holy Spirit." WOORTMANN, Klaas. *Religion and Science in the Renaissance*, p. 115.

[18] HOOYKAAS, R. *The Religion and Development of Modern Science*, pp. 162-169.

[19] GALILEO. *Dialogues Concerning the Two New Sciences*. Trad. Ing. H. Crew and A. de Salvio. Chicago: Encyclopedia Britannica, 1980.

[20] "Galileo and Kepler, two of the founders of modern science, believed, like Plato, that God, in creating the world, acted in accordance with mathematical models. There was, however, an essential difference between his point of view and that of the great Greek philosopher. Plato believed that matter was a hindrance so that the Mathematical Ideas could be accurately reflected in the world of phenomena [...] In turn, Galileo and Kepler believed that the Creator fully realized His mathematical plan of the universe., for them, the experience was not irrelevant." Ibid., pp. 56-57.

[21] "Even Bacon's 'incomprehension' toward Gilbert arises from the ground of a

William Gilbert (1544-1603) studied magnetism and electricity. He understood the magnetism of the Earth. Using the compass, he believed he could prove this, for the needle of the instrument was drawn towards north. Gilbert, who was English, was appointed physician to Elizabeth I, Queen of England, whose policy provided a golden era for the country.

All these thinkers and scientists, who preceded or were contemporaries of Bacon, strove to study reality and promote knowledge without disregarding mysticism. Bacon joined this tradition by valuing nature's experimentation. He proceeded on the path established by these men, revealing to the world the great works that experimental study could produce, whether for the intellectual or social life.[22]

2.2 *Mysticism and Cosmology in Bacon*

There was a good deal of speculation concerning Bacon's rejection of the alchemists and Hermeticists in favor of a science that pioneered modern mechanics. Is this generalization correct? No. In the first place, Bacon did not perceive alchemy to be wrong. He merely preferred that the transmutation of elements into gold should be seriously considered only after this idea had passed through the sieve of the true inductive method.[23] Secondly, the Hermetic

---

positioning against the 'magical' and hermetizing theses present in *De magnete*. Gilbert defends the movement of the Earth, but is not absolutely disposed to follow Copernicus in the thesis of a rotation of the Earth around the sun [...] and writes pages that aim to sustain, with references to Hermes, Zoroaster, Orfeu, the doctrine of universal animation." WOORTMANN, Klaas. *Religion and Science in the Renaissance*, p. 59.

[22] "In this framework of scholastic culture, Bacon had resumed the themes that had characterized the anti-Aristotelian and anti-scholastic literature of the late Middle Ages, Humanism, and the Renaissance. For Bacon also, as for Agricola, Vives, Nizolio, Ramus, Patrizi, scholasticism coincides with the predominance of Aristotelianism, with the reduction of the entire field of knowledge to logic, with the exhaustion of logical research to a series of distinctions that cannot become cognitive instruments in means capable of carrying out *operations* on the natural reality." ROSSI, Paolo. *Francis Bacon: From Magic to Science*, pp. 191-192.

[23] BACON, Francis. *Novum Organum* [1620]. Trad. br. José Aluysio Reis de

tradition is too complex to be defined without the careful study of particular instances and the exceptions from it. Bacon did not rule out the empirical validity of all Hermetic studies, only those he believed to be grounded in prejudices and superstitions. According to Rusu, Della Porta's work *Magia Naturalis* exerted considerable influence on the project of *Sylva Sylvarum*. For Wigston, "Bacon's writings suggest a deep intimacy with Hermetic science and with the mysteries of antiquity [...] Bacon [also] studied the Egyptian, Persian, and Chaldean myths."[24]

According to Sophie Weeks, in her doctoral thesis entitled *Francis Bacon's Science of Magic*, Bacon's criticism of Bernardino Telesio (1509-1588), whom Bacon called "the first of the moderns", was not due to the presence of occult elements in that author, but rather his rejection of the Telesian understanding of nature, which used the hot and cold categories—respectively representing expansion and contraction—to study the heavens and the earth and to perceive totality from dichotomies such as "mobility and immobility," "rarity and density," and "light and darkness." According to Bacon, Telesio had improved the philosophy of the Peripatetics, the disciples of Aristotle, but had not gone very far.[25] Bacon, for example, was no different from Cornelius Agrippa (1483-1535) when, in *De occulta philosophia libri tres*, he says that the natural world, which for him was composed of the four elements (water, air, earth, and fire)—was knowable and interrelated—for Agrippa, the four elements are related to the mineral, metallic, vegetal, and animal spheres of nature.[26] Bacon saw nature as reality, capable of being understood, and thought that its distinct spheres could be joined together as an epistemological whole.

Andrade. São Paulo: Abril Cultural, 1984, p. 96.

[24] WIGSTON, W. F. C. *Bacon, Shakespeare, and the Rosicrucians*. London: Tübner and Co., 1884, p. xix.

[25] WEEKS, Sophie Vitoria. *Francis Bacon's Science of Magic*. Leeds: University of Leeds, 2007, pp. 55-56.

[26] AGRIPPA, Cornelius. *Three Books of Occult Philosophy - Book I*. USA: Hermetics, 2000, p.11.

He also shared with Agrippa the appreciation of Democritus (460-370 BC), who was considered by Bacon as superior to the Greek philosophers that came after Socrates (469-399 BC). In spite of the possible differences in the concept of induction, both Bacon and Agrippa wanted to understand the absolute reality that was "behind" the particular phenomena which "conceals" nature to the "naked eye" and can be perceived by the application of appropriate method.

Investigating Bacon's analysis of the Cupid myth, Weeks argues that Bacon claims this myth, wherein primordial love has united with chaos and generated the gods, reveals the original impulse of the atom, acting as chaos and organizing the world, which Bacon believes to be creation *ex chao*.[27] It is worth noting, however, that Bacon suggests the prospect of God being an inexplicable creator. If this argument is considered valid, then there are some implications for the notion that there is a real continuity between Mystic-Hermetic thinking and Baconian thinking:

1. Bacon departs from the notion of the *creato ex nihilo* of Thomas Aquinas, as well as of the Thomistic notion of *Analogia Entis*, and is closer to the Greek and pagan cosmogony of the world than this;

2. His attempt to reconcile faith in God with *creato ex chao* makes his Christianity closer to the Negative Way of the mystical tradition of Pseudo-Dionysian Areopagite, Christian Cabala and the notion of uncreated light,[28] and *theosis*[29] in the mystical Christianity of the Eastern world;

3. If the atom is not caused, while reality is not reduced to pure materialism, Bacon follows the non-dualist

---

[27] WEEKS, Sophie Vitoria. *Francis Bacon's Science of Magic*, pp.68-72.

[28] In the Eastern Christian idea of uncreated light, divine energy is literally united with the space-time world, so that the uncreated reality of energies, called "light," can "join" or even "penetrate" the created thing.

[29] *Theosis* is, in Eastern Christianity, the idea that through participation in the divine energies, or uncreated light, man can "deify" himself, in the sense of uniting himself, without confusion of natures, with the divine.

monistic tradition of certain Hermetic writers and Eastern traditions.

All of this implies that there was continuity between the mystical tradition of the Renaissance and Bacon's philosophy, although its inductive method required the freedom to break with the errors of the past to make progress. It turns out that, according to Weeks, there is in Bacon a recreation *ex chao*.[30] Because there is no "cause" of the primordial atom, the Baconian inductive method itself, striving towards new knowledge and progress, "recreates" the thing as it is known. *Compositio* is the nature of the thing before being used by the inductive method. *Mistio* is the thing "modified" by method. This modification, however, is not to be an annihilation of its previous nature, but a "re-creation", in the sense that, as the thing progresses, "progress" becomes "new" and it must be allowed to continue in its simpler state, while the complexity, which is new, modifies it. In this way the progress achieved by the method always conserves and transmutes, acting magically yet still sharing the same substratum.[31]

2.2.1 PAN, CUPID, MAGIC, AND GRAVITATION

Wang[32] argues that there is an overestimation of Gilbert's (1544-1603) work on gravitation and an underestimation of Bacon's contribution to the same theme. It is commonly thought that Gilbert's theses on magnetism, electricity, and attraction influenced Wren (1632-1723), Wilkins, Wallis, Hooke (1635-103), and Newton (1643-1727). For Wang, however, some errors need to be remedied when it comes to analyzing the degree of this influence. First, Wang interprets Gilbert as advocating a kind of influence of the Earth on the celestial bodies that were "material," that is, using the concept of *effluvium*, with small invisible particles that electrically attracted the bodies. Wang

---

[30] WEEKS, Vitoria. *Francis Bacon's Science of Magic*, pp. 258, 266.

[31] To delve into Bacon's investigation of the Cupid myth, see Bacon, Francis. *The Wisdom of the Ancients*. Trad. br. Gilson César Cardoso de Souza. São Paulo: UNESP, 2002, pp. 56-60.

[32] See WANG, Xiaona. *Francis Bacon's Magic and the Universal Principle of Gravitation*. Francis Bacon Society, Baconiana, Volume 1, No. 6, 2009, England, p. 1.

states that Gilbert's separation of magnetism and electricity does not alter the fact that he clearly denied the possibility of the attraction of the bodies at a distance. For Gilbert, the attraction would be for the "touch." Now, since Hooke, Wren, and Newton advocate the attraction of bodies at a distance, the attraction without a "touch," Gilbert cannot have influenced them in this regard. In addition, Gilbert did not believe that magnetism was an attractive force, while Wallis, Wilkins, and Hooke, did. Bacon is then pointed to as the influence for the thesis of distant attraction by these authors and of the Baconian notion of magnetism. Wang shows that, unlike Gilbert, Bacon supported attraction at a distance, but without the invisible particles in Gilbert's *effluvium* theory. He also argued that the attraction of bodies is similar to magnetism. In this Wang includes Voltaire (1694-1778), who had already claimed to be a precursor of the Newtonian thesis on gravity. Wang concludes that it was Bacon and not Gilbert who was more influential for Newton and other members of the Royal Society.

That said, the questions remain: if the attraction of bodies is not a "touch," as Gilbert wanted, but is done at a distance, what attracts the bodies? What is the "magnetic attraction" for Bacon? Wang says the answer is found in the Baconian idea of magic. This distinguishes Bacon from other authors of the Royal Society. Bacon believed in the possibility that magical forces could attract bodies. The attraction at a distance would be similar to magnetism, but it would not be exactly like the universal gravitation that Newton later postulated, rather a magico-magnetic attraction of the Earth on the bodies, the moon on the tides, and the celestial spheres on the movement of the planets. Wang points out that this thesis is similar to that of the Arab philosopher Al-Kindi that all things are influenced by radios[33]

---

[33] On Al-Kindi's philosophy, Couliano says: "The doctrine of conjunctions, derived from Al-Kindi and Albumasar, was associated with various theories of the cosmic cycles formulated by Roger Bacon, Peter of Abano, Abbot Trithemo, Adam Nachemoser, Kepler, and others. There is no perfect agreement between them, but all are based on the Al-Kindi dating, which the German folklorist Will Erich Peukert (1895-1969) summarizes as follows: the conjunction of the higher planets is repeated every 20 years; it changes 4 times, succeeding among the signs of a triangle; finally, at the end of 240 years, it passes to the next triangle, in the order of the signs, and repeats the cycle; the same happens in the 3rd and 4th

(understood here not in the modern, reduced sense). Bacon uses the notion of rays[34] in his analysis of the myth of Pan, which would be nature:

> The body of Nature is represented in an elegant and true way, all covered with hairs, alluding to the rays that all bodies emit (in fact, the rays resemble the hair or bristles of nature, and almost nothing exists that is no longer or me radiant). This can easily be seen in the power of vision, and not least in the various kinds of magnetic virtue, or in phenomena that occur at a distance (for anything that produces effect at a distance must undoubtedly emit rays). However, Pan's hair is longer in the beard because the rays of the celestial bodies operate and penetrate a greater distance than any other ...[35]

Already the actions at a distance are accepted in their analysis of the myth of Cupid, as follows:

> Finally, Cupid is archer, that is, his virtue consists in acting at a distance (because all operation at a distance resembles the throwing of the arrow). Who, therefore, supports the theory of the atom and of the vacuum (although it does not suppose the latter segregated in itself but widespread), implicitly maintains

---

triangles. After 4 times 240 years 1484 (960), it returns to the starting point, the first sign of the first triangle, in the same degree of the beginning, passes to the next degree and begins a new cycle. There are, therefore, three periods or cycles: 1. The small cycle, of 20 years duration, between two conjunctions. 2. The average cycle, of 240 years duration, from one triangle to another. 3. The great cycle, of 960 years duration, lasting until the return of the conjunction of the same place in the zodiac. The last, which is almost a millennium, marks a complete renewal of the world, which involves a new particular religion. The middle cycle confines great political agitations, changes in government, etc. Finally, the small cycle usually indicates important events, real successions, revolutions and other crises of state." COULIANO, Ioan. *Eros and Magic in Renaissance*. Translated to English by Margaret Cook. London: University Chicago Press, 1987, pp. 186-187.

[34] Bacon also knew the pyramidal form of fire. See *Descriptio Globi Intellectualis*. BACON, Francis. *The Philosophical Works of Francis Bacon*. New York: Routledge, 2011, p. 699.

[35] BACON, Francis. *The Wisdom of the Ancients*, pp. 34-35.

that the virtue of the atom operates at a distance – since, without this, no motion would originate, for cause of the vacuum brought, all things being fixed and immobile.[36]

If Wang's interpretation can be challenged and his appreciation of Bacon's work questioned, one thing becomes indisputable: the notion of magic was present in Bacon's intellectual assumptions, and that for him magic was science, and science—being magical—was true. The magical explanation and the scientific explanation would not be explanations coming from two different fields, but one and the same magical-scientific or simply scientific explanation.

2.3 Bacon and the Mystery Schools

Pizzinga advocates for the truthfulness of the fact that Bacon was a Rosicrucian, exercising in this mystery school the role of Imperator and writing the Rosicrucian manifestos *Fama Fraternitatis* (1614), *Confessio Fraternitatis* (1615), and *Die Chymische Hochzeit Christiani Rosencreutz* (1616). To know if all this is true or not is beyond the scope of this work. What makes this statement very relevant, however, is that Pizzinga, along with other scholars of mysticism, esoterism, and magic, sees evidence of a mysticism compatible with that of the Rosicrucian and other mystery schools in Bacon. There are parallels that need to be highlighted. The Baconian project of the Instauratio Magna, for example, is seen as an esoteric project of mastery of the cosmos by knowledge, in which the Gnostic tradition would be called enlightenment and dominion by *gnosis*.[37] Bacon's words make clear the idea of dominance in his project on knowledge:

> The true and legitimate goal of science is to endow human life with new inventions and resources. Science and [...]

---

[36] Ibid., p. 59.

[37] Although gnosis is not a word of the Baconian vocabulary, we will now speak of gnosis in Bacon's thought to emphasize the similarity between his ideas and the Gnostic and Hermetic mysteries.

human power coincides, since the cause is ignored, the effect is thwarted. For nature cannot be overcome, except when it is obeyed [...] Man, the minister and interpreter of nature, does and understands as much as he finds.[38]

Such dominion by knowledge—or gnosis—is exemplified in even more detail, for Pizzinga, in the Baconian allegory of the House of Solomon. White seems to agree. He says, "The House of Solomon represents a kind of initiation,"[39] and, continuing, "That Bacon intended the *New Atlantis* to signify the Promised Land is quite clear."[40]

This science, understood here not as modern science, but as knowledge which illuminates the domain of the cosmos, is aimed at the restoration of the Empire of Man, of the empire of knowledge, or, in a sense, of the empire of gnosis. Man is at the top of the cosmos, he is the great initiate, the great master, unsurpassed only by God.

In *New Atlantis*, every twelve years, three men were sent out of the island of Bensalem on two ships to collect information about other peoples. The numerology of *New Atlantis* is seen as cabalist, since twelve is a special number in this school. Moreover, Pizzinga asserts (1) that the Baconian concepts of knowledge and action are associated with the esoteric categories of positive (active) and negative (theoretical) polarity; 2) that because Bacon regards sulfur and mercury as the primary elements of nature he can be considered an author who has used the triadic alchemist concepts of fire (sulfur), water (mercury), and the fusion and transmutation thereof. Pizzinga also speculates on the totality of the numerical meanings existing in *New Atlantis*, in which one group is composed of the number twelve and all the others by the number three, which, for Pizzinga, can represent, by calculations, "manifestation of perfect harmony" (3), "image of the three worlds" (3 + 3 + 3) and "complete and perfect harmony" (12). This is allied to the fact that the figures of

---

[38] BACON, Francis. *Novum Organum* [1620], pp. 48, 13.
[39] STRAUSS. Leo; CROPSEY, Joseph. *History of Political Philosophy*. Francis Bacon Section. Chicago: University of Chicago Press, 1987, p. 377.
[40] Ibid., p. 375.

Solomon and of the temple were, and continue to be used by, various schools of mysteries, including modern Freemasonry. Although Pizzinga's considerations may not be suitable for some – who see more rupture than continuity between Bacon and the Renaissance mystics, hardly any of the similarities he has raised between Bacon and esotericism can be considered unfounded[41] or unworthy of academic consideration.

2.4 Mysticism in New Atlantis

Bacon understands that self-knowledge cannot be dissociated from the knowledge of the totality of the cosmos. This is more comprehensive, so that only when integrated into the totality of the cosmos is self-knowledge effective. Therefore, rather than a knowledge restricted to the individual, self-knowledge is a portion of natural knowledge:

> We now come to this knowledge to which the ancient oracle, which is the knowledge of ourselves, leads us to this knowledge... This knowledge, being the end and end of natural philosophy in the intention of man, is not, however, a portion of the natural philosophy if one considers with respect to the totality of the nature.[42]

In her book *Francis Bacon and His Secret Society*, Mrs. Pott argues that the belief that Bacon was one of the founders of the Rosicrucian Brotherhood[43] may find grounds for comparing Baconian aspirations

---

[41] PIZZINGA. R. *The Thought of a Legendary Imperator Rosacruz Sir Francis Bacon - On the College of the Work of the Six Days of the Island of Bensalem*. Public Monograph, Svmmvm Bonvm Organization. This monograph of Dr. Pizzinga is available to the public through the electronic address http://www.revistaartereal.com.br/wp-content/uploads/2014/02/o-pensamento-de-francis-bacon-rD-Pizzinga.pdf.

[42] BACON, Francis. *The Advancement of Learning* [1605]. Trad. br. Raul Fiker. São Paulo: UNESP, 2007, p. 167.

[43] Influential esoteric confraternity among European intellectuals during the

with those of this fraternity, which are sometimes identical. Mrs. Pott says:

> Comparing the statements of the alleged authors of the Rosicrucian manifestos with Bacon's statements reiterated the statements as their own visions and aspirations. We find them identical in thought and feeling, sometimes identical in expression.[44]

Mrs. Pott further emphasizes the purpose of the fraternity:

1. To purify religion and to encourage reformation in the church;
2. to promote and improve knowledge and science;
3. to mitigate the miseries of humanity and to restore man to his original state of purity and happiness to which he fell by sin.[45]

Any balanced reader of Bacon will be able to see that, in fact, such purposes are very similar to the Baconian project of Instauratio Magna from true science. Like Pizzinga, Mrs. Pott also claims to see an esoteric character in *New Atlantis*. She even compares the centrality of sunlight in *New Atlantis* with the sentence of Hermes Trismegistus, "I am that light, Pure Intelligence, thy God," as well as the Rosicrucian statement: "Where also God, when matter was prepared by the love of the light, gives his Fiat Lux, which was not creation, as the majority thinks, but a Word, in which was life and that life which is the light of man."[46] Mrs. Pott also considers *New Atlantis* as similar to the Rosicrucian *Journey to the Land of the Rosicrucians*.[47] Mrs. Pott's work, therefore, seeks to show that such similarities are more than mere coincidences and that there

---

sixteenth and seventeenth centuries.

[44] POTT, Mrs. Henry. *Francis Bacon and his Secret Society*. Chicago: J. Schult and Company, 1891, pp. 204.

[45] Ibid., p. 204.

[46] Ibid., p. 337.

[47] See Ibid., p. 329.

is evidence to suggest that Bacon was not only a magician[48] and a mystic,[49] but also a key element in the creation and development of mystery schools such as the Rosicrucians.

McKnight argues that in *New Atlantis* the land of Bensalem has a spirituality superior to that of Christian Europe. Even if it is a spirituality with Christian roots, for McKnight, there is a purity and perfection in Bensalem from knowledge, which perhaps no people previously established under this (Christian) religion ever experienced. Contrasting Europe and Bensalem, one might even say that heaven with its angelic inhabitants, so long sought by the Europeans, seems to be united with Bensalem so that the wise can be related to the angels. If this interpretation is possible, there is more evidence for gnosis and Hermeticism in Bacon, since many mystics of these schools argue that enlightenment reveals the secrets of the heavenly and the angelic world. White asserts: "The most important myth for Bacon [*New Atlantis*] is [...] partly a creation of its own and partly a refutation of the Platonic myth [...] the history of Atlantis, an island somewhere from the west, reaches us in Plato, is the story of the technological paradise."[50] White continues: "Bacon deliberately puts the myth of Plato upside down. He admits that ancient Atlantis was destroyed, but by a flood [not by an earthquake], suggesting that there are also mountain peoples who survived and then built the

---

[48] Zaterka says: "Bacon was certainly inspired by several mid-century thinkers. XVI and early seventeenth century to elaborate his theory of matter. Among the most important, we can highlight Paracelsus, Telésio, Campanella, and Gilbert, the first being the most striking influence." *The Experimental Philosophy in Eighteenth-Century England: Francis Bacon and Robert Boyle*, pp. 114-115.

[49] A mystical view of nature, which possesses a hidden truth, which in itself is superior to the intellect, is found in the following passage of the *Novum Organum*: "The true cause and root of all evils affecting the sciences is a single one: while we admire and falsely exalt the powers of the human mind, we do not seek adequate aid to it [...] Nature overcomes in a great deal, in complexity, the senses and the intellect. All those beautiful meditations and human speculations, all controversies are unhealthy things. And no one notices it." BACON, Francis. *Novum Organum* [1620], p. 14.

[50] STRAUSS. Leo; CROPSEY, Joseph. *History of Political Philosophy*. Francis Bacon Section, pp. 375-376.

Inca and Mayan civilizations."[51] He concludes further that "Bacon's *New Atlantis* seems to suggest a certain civil religion, [represented] in a festival which is called the feast of Tirsan [...] [This] feast is a mixture of pagan feasts [...] Its symbols suggest Osiris and Isis, Egyptian deities."[52]

With these interpretations of *New Atlantis*, the question arises: Could the work just be utopian genre literature, as has been suggested? McKnight shows that authors such as White and Weinberger, finding that Bacon possessed a conception of reality that endorsed the need for a real separation between the creed and the political world, believed that Bacon "used" religious language not as a "believer", but instead for political purposes.[53] This finding, however, is incomplete. The mystic does not perform this kind of separation, eliminating any form of religious message from a symbolic work, even if this work has political ends. Neither the mythical, symbolical, or creedal world is confined to the ritual sphere of religion, but rather embraces the entire spiritual worldview of the world. In other words, for the mystic, it is not possible to separate politics from the spirit, and symbolism expresses a metaphysical reality hidden from the practical and social world. Therefore, before even considering the prospect that *New Atlantis* is a politically and literary utopian work, there remains the assertion that it is also a mystical work, as indicated by "[the Rosicrucian] John Heydon ... [who] identifies the *New Atlantis* of Bacon as the 'Land of the Rosicrucians.'"[54] A similar interpretation of this was provided by Yates.[55] One could, however, counter-claim that Bacon could not be a mystic author since he was a critic of Platonic thought, which influenced many Renaissance mystics. Although this argument is good, it does not hold. McKnight correctly argues that *New Atlantis* is influenced by Plato himself (428

---

[51] Ibid., p. 376.

[52] Ibid., p. 378.

[53] MCKNIGHT, Stephen A. *The Religious Foundations of Francis Bacon's Thought*. Eric Voegelin Institute Series in Political Philosophy: Studies in Religion and Politics. Columbia: University of Missouri Press, 2006, p. 74.

[54] WIGSTON, W. F. C. *Bacon, Shakespeare and the Rosicrucians*, p. XVIII.

[55] CLARK, Stuart. *Thinking with Demons: The History of Witchcraft in the Beginning of Modern Europe*. Trad. br. Celso Mauro Paciornik. EDUSP, São Paulo, 1997, p. 295.

-348 BC), specifically by the works *Timaeus* and *Critias*.⁵⁶ Bacon used the belief of many ancient peoples in a primordial paradise, such as the idea of a Golden Age or lost Atlantis (which Plato used in his dialogues), to defend a theological-political or even mystical-political position: *New Atlantis* would be the restoration of the Golden Age, the rediscovery (or even overcoming) of Atlantis, and the eschatological glory achieved by scientific knowledge (gnosis). In addition to the prominence of Solomon in the work—who is also a key figure in the Renaissance influenced by Plato—it is clear that Bacon was not afraid of being confused with the mystical disciples of Plato or sympathizers of the Greek philosopher.⁵⁷

Another important point must be emphasized in the investigation of the mysticism of *New Atlantis*: Bacon's interest in the mysticism of Judea. Why is this? Because not every mystic has relations with Christian mysticism, Renaissance mysticism, the Rosicrucian movement, Jewish mysticism, and modern Freemasonry. White does not overlook the fact that "[an] official [of Solomon's House] wears the tunic of the Old Testament High Priest."⁵⁸ McKnight also highlights the figure of the Jew Joabin in *New Atlantis*, who for him may be a reference to Joab, commander of the army of King David, the father of Solomon.⁵⁹ Joabin is present in Bacon's work and is an important figure for the House of Solomon. They represent a patriarchal model of society, and the people of Bensalem are considered to be descendants of Abraham, who received the

---

⁵⁶ See MCKNIGHT, Stephen A. *The Religious Foundations of Francis Bacon's Thought*, p. 75.

⁵⁷ "So long as philosophers are not kings in cities, or those whom we now call kings and sovereigns, are not truly and seriously philosophers, so long as political power and philosophy do not converge in the same individual, while the many characters who now pursue one or other of these sole objectives are not prevented from doing so, my dear Glaucus will have no end, the evils of the cities, nor, as I judge, of the human kind, and the city which we have described will never be built." PLATO. *Republic*. Trad. of Maria Helena da Rocha Pereira. Lisbon: Gulbenkian, 1983.

⁵⁸ STRAUSS. Leo; CROPSEY, Joseph. *History of Political Philosophy*. Francis Bacon Section, pp. 377.

⁵⁹ MCKNIGHT, Stephen A. *The Religious Foundations of Francis Bacon's Thought*, p. 84.

laws of Moses. This forms a basis for arguing that Bacon viewed the Jewish wisdom tradition with respect even after the advent of Christianity. This corroborates with the fact that the Calvinist spirit present, which was present in England is less critical of Judaism than traditional Catholicism. This, however, did not necessarily make Bacon's attitude toward Judaism antagonistic to its historical-social context. It is worth remembering that symbolic language was seen by Bacon as a way in which the ancients transmitted knowledge. This thought is in tune with Jewish esoteric thinking, important to modern Freemasonry, and in other secret societies. According to them, Solomon, the wisest man in the world, transmitted secret knowledge through symbols so that only the most capable initiates could understand them. Here are the words of Bacon:

> The earliest and earliest investigators of the truth, with more fidelity and success, used to record in the form of aphorisms, that is, brief individual decisions not bound by any methodological artifice, the knowing that they gathered from the observation of things and intended to preserve them for later use.[60]

The following figure indicates, for some, the idea of supernovae as symbols of change. These supernovae, present in the celestial bodies, illuminate the temple, the place of initiates (and enlightened ones) in true knowledge-gnosis. Ball says that "Heydon more or less equates the House of Solomon with the Rose-cross Temple."[61]

---

[60] BACON, Francis. *Novum Organum* [1620], pp. 94-95.

[61] BALL, Phillip. *Curiosity: How Science Became Interested in Everything*. USA: University of Chicago Press, 2012, p. 82. The figure can be studied at the site: http://www.adventuresofnicky.com/blog/371_oak-island-and-the-rosicrucian-star-of wisdom.html

THE MYSTICAL FOUNDATIONS OF FRANCIS BACON'S SCIENCE

Figure 1 - The Rose Cross Temple, by Theophilus Schweighardt Constantiens, 1618.[62]

---

[62] See JONES, Marie; FIAXMAN, Larry. *Viral Mythology: How the Truth of the Ancients was Encoded and Passed Down*. USA: The Career Press, 2014.

The use of mythical and symbolic language by Bacon was not limited to *New Atlantis*. In *The Wisdom of the Ancients*, Bacon investigated the wisdom hidden behind the various lyrical and poetic myths of antiquity. Even in *Novum Organum*, mythology is important. MacIntyre, in *Francis Bacon's Use of Ancient Myth in Novum Organum* says: "The ancient myths of Pan, Perseus, Dionysius, and Prometheus have an impact on Book I of Francis Bacon's *Novum Organum*."[63] Again, it is argued that Bacon longs for science to return to the Golden Age or, in theological language, to the pre-lapsarian state prior to the Fall, when everything was perfect: "myths/fables, in Bacon's view, could make man return to his pre-lapsarian state and return his power over created things to him."[64]

MacIntyre believes that Pan, for Bacon, symbolizes nature, and an openness and invitation to knowledge to the detriment of those who, absent from nature, are bound to the Idol of the Cave. The figure of Pegasus, a symbol of victory in war, which emerges from the head of Medusa after being killed by Perseus, has the gift of flying through the natural world, representing the "flight" or investigation that is undertaken in order to know the whole of reality.[65] Perseus, in MacIntyre's analysis, is also important. To defeat Medusa, Perseus used various instruments, given by Hermes, Hades, Athena, and the Graeae. Just as Perseus needed instruments, the scientist, for Bacon, needs the inductive method. Just as Perseus overcame Medusa with them, as well as being able to fly with his instruments of war, the scientist must use the inductive method to dominate nature and "fly." MacIntyre also relates the myth of Dionysus and ivy with *Novum Organum*. Besides being a wine god, Dionysus is known as a giver of peace and joy. The ivy, in turn, represents strength and endurance, despite the dangers of winter. In this sense, ivy would represent the effort and determination gained by the use of methodology over nature, and Dionysus would represent peace

---

[63] MACINTYRE, Wendell. *Francis Bacon's Use of Ancient Myth in Novum Organum*. University of Prince Edward Island, Alicantina Journal of British Studies 7 (1994): 123-32, England, p. 123.

[64] Ibid., p. 124.

[65] See Ibid., p. 124.

and joy from the enlightenment when the scientist arrives with the knowledge of reality.⁶⁶ Another example by MacIntyre uses the myth of Prometheus.

As Prometheus possesses powers that give hope to humanity, MacIntyre interprets it as symbolizing the stimulus to the search for truth and the hope that it will be achieved by the inductive method. Moreover, since Prometheus is associated with the origin of fire in the world, he can also symbolize the light that illuminates knowledge.⁶⁷

2.5 Hermeticism, Neoplatonism, and Monism in Bacon

Paolo Rossi (1923-2012) agrees with the authors mentioned here about the influence of magical thinking on Bacon.⁶⁸ Indeed, in his book *Francis Bacon: From Magic to Science*, Rossi shows that this magic should not be understood as mere superstition, nor even as contrary to the desire for rigorous empirical methods, but instead as an understanding of the world from a pre-modern and pre-mechanic perspective.⁶⁹ These mystics did not make magic in the pejorative sense that this term implied after the advent of modern science. "Magic" is now synonymous with unscientific beliefs and superstitions – instead they used science in the full sense of the word. They did not experience the phenomena sociologist Max Weber (1864-1920) would later call the disenchantment of the world

---

⁶⁶ Ibid. pp. 129-130.

⁶⁷ See Ibidem, p. 130-131.

⁶⁸ Rossi states: "From the great tradition of Renaissance magic – which reached its maximum splendor in the years between the activity of Marsilius Ficino and that of Campanella and Robert Fludd (between the middle of the fifteenth century and the thirties of the seventeenth century) the moderns have embraced a central idea: knowledge is not only contemplation of truth, but it is also power, dominion over nature, an attempt to prolong its work to subject it to the needs and aspirations of man. But this theme–haunted in the magical-hermetic tradition– was inserted in a discourse that decisively rejected the image of the sage and note of knowledge that served as background to the hermetic culture." ROSSI, Paolo. *Shipwrecks Without Spectators: The Idea of Progress*. Trad. br. Álvaro Lorencini. São Paulo: UNESP, 2000, p. 48.

⁶⁹ See ROSSI, Paolo. *Francis Bacon: From Magic to Science*, pp. 191-192.

in modernity. Matter and spirit were not antagonistic. Behind the natural was the spiritual. To discover the hidden truth through visible phenomena was the function of the scientist, who, precisely because he was a scientist, was mystical. Bacon, for example, believed in the science of physiognomies. Porter attests[70] that in the eyes of Lord Verulam "the art of physiognomy was the *science* that dealt with the 'bond' or common bond of the soul and body, 'which makes [man] united and indivisible nature.'" Porter continues:

> Especially considering the similarities and concordances between soul and body, [he] knew that if mixed, they could not be studied by any science. Physiognomy was, therefore, a 'genuine portion of natural philosophy.'[71]

Furthermore, "[for the English philosopher, physiognomy was] 'sister' of the art of dream interpretation and capable of contributing to 'self-knowledge' or, in other words, to fulfill the ancient oracle: '*Nosce teipsum*, know thyself.'"[72] The belief in sympathy was not alien to Bacon either. He described a sympathy of his day that would use the viola and music, so that "sympathy operates as well by the transmission of sound as by movement."[73] Concerning the evil eye, he said, "We see, just as the Scriptures call envy the eye of evil [...] [Proverbs 23: 6; 28,22], seeming to recognize in the act of envy an ejaculation or irradiation of the eye."[74] The spirit, in addition, was seen as being in direct relation to matter and body: "We must investigate how much spirit and how much tangible essence there is in every body, and whether that spirit is copious and turgid or jejunum and whether it is tenuous or thick, whether it is closer to air

---

[70] Porter, Martin. *Windows of the Soul: Physiognomy in European Culture 1470-1780*. New York: Oxford University Press, 2005, p. 169.

[71] Ibidem, p. 169.

[72] Ibid., p. 169.

[73] BACON, *Sylva Sylvarum* apud SCHLIESSER, Eric. *Sympathy: A History*. New York: Oxford University Press, 2015, p. 103.

[74] BACON, *Novum Organum* apud ZATERKA, Luciana. *The Theories of Matter by Francis Bacon and Robert Boyle: Shape, Texture, and Activity*. scientiæ zudia, v. 10, n. 4, p. 681-709, São Paulo, 2012, p. 688.

or fire, whether it is active or apathetic, whether it is thin or robust, whether in progress or in return." Similarly, "The same must be done in relation to the tangible essence and its fibers, fibers and their multiple structures, as well as the placement of the spirits in the substance and its pores, conduits, veins, and cells and the rudiments or attempts of the organic body."[75]

Although Bacon was critical of alchemists and Hermeticists, there was no reason for Rossi to prematurely reject any considerations made by these Renaissance thinkers. Bacon was indeed an influence of the Renaissance spirit, which not only greatly influenced empirical research, but also breathed new life into debates on logic and rhetoric. Rossi highlights the fact that, in addition to being influenced by the mystic, Bacon was a *ramista*,[76] a disciple of the logical and rhetorical humanist critic of Aristotelian logic, Pedro Ramo (1515-1572).

It turns out that even Ramist humanism, whose teaching on logic, thought it was necessary to undo the exaggerations and complications of Aristotelian logic, in order to make logic accessible to a larger number of people and no longer just to an elite group. This stood out in the wake of Renaissance anti-Aristotelianism. It is not naive to think that rebirth, humanism, and Protestantism, in one way or another, participated together in the late Middle Ages and the beginning of Modernity. Opposition to Aristotle in the late Middle Ages united all these groups. Bacon walked a path between humanism, Protestantism, and mysticism. As anti-Aristotelian,

---

[75] BACON apud AGRIPPA. *Three Books of Religious Philosophy*. Trad. br. Marcos Malvezzi. pp. 151-152.

[76] Concerning the teachings of Ramus, Althusius says: "The law [*ramist*] of justice (*lex justitiae*) indicates that every art or science has its own purpose, and that such an objective serves as a principle for the determination of what is suitable for each art (*suum cuique*), and that everything that is not appropriate must be strictly excluded [...] The *ramista* law of truth (*lex veritatis*) indicates that an art or science consists of universal and necessary propositions or precepts, and that those which are only true in certain places and on certain occasions must be separated... The ramistic law of wisdom (*lex sapientiae*) indicates that a proposition must be placed in the nearest class of things to which it belongs, rather than being in matters of greater or lesser degree of generality." ALTHUSIUS, Johannes. *Politics*. Trad. Joubert de Oliveira Brízida. Rio de Janeiro: Topbooks Editora, 2003, pp. 15-16.

he was also able to use varied sources that opposed the Greek philosopher.

Faced with these facts, the question arises: How did Bacon see the world? Did he see a disenchanted world, to use Max Weber's words, or, as a pre-modern man, did he see an enchanted world? If it is said that Bacon has already seen the world with the eyes of a modern man, it would be necessary to make a historical revision of all the influence of mysticism and religion on his thought. If it were said that he simply saw the enchanted world, as a vulgar man would see it, he would have to disregard all his criticism of the ancients, his appeal to method, to progress, and his defense of the "new." A simple answer to this question, therefore, does not exist. However, it is possible to make some important considerations in this regard. In the first place, Bacon was not a skeptical materialist, as many modern scientists have become since modern science broke with a past that he considered superstitious. Secondly, Bacon believed the existence of truth, which was not agnostic, like many in modernity.

For him, what the average man understood by nature was only the superficial manifestation of something that had to be unveiled by the scientific method. In this sense, science and the occult come together.[77] It is noteworthy that Japiassu arrives at a similar conclusion. In his book *Francis Bacon: The Prophet of Modern Science*, Japiassu traces the relationship between science and occultism in *The Hidden Face of Modern Science*. This relationship between truth, nature, inductive method, and concealment leads to another question: mystical monism. It is wrong to treat every monistic approach to the world as pantheistic or atheistic. This reduction to monism, which for example, fails to understand monistic schools such as the *advaita vedanta*,[78] whose monism cannot be reduced to the pantheism of the

---

[77] Popper states: "Bacon substituted 'God' for 'Nature'. This may be the reason why we need to purify ourselves before we approach the goddess Natura: once our mind is purified, even our senses, which do not always deserve trust (and which Plato considers totally unclean), become clear. The sources of knowledge need to be kept pure because any impurity can turn them into sources of ignorance ... I do not think, however, that Bacon [...] succeeded in liberating authority [his epistemology]. POPPER, Karl. *Conjectures and Refutations*. Trad. br. Sérgio Bath. Brasília: UNB, 1972, pp. 43, 118.

[78] Hindu monist school.

Spinozian school, and unlike Spinoza (1632-1677), who was expelled from the Jewish community, has no harmful implications for the preservation of religious tradition.

On the contrary, the Vedanta school is not seen by its adherents as contrary to the belief in transcendence, in the sense of reducing it to immanence, but of considering it under a paradigm that gives immanent reality the possibility of overcoming itself, of transcending itself, without annihilating the substance from which things emanate. Similarly, Sufi mystics, the mystical wing of Islam, and Eastern Christians, principally through the teaching of *Theosis* and through the practice of Hesychasm,[79] are not dualistic in the Platonic sense, nor strongly influenced by Aristotelian logic, do not use Western metaphysics to deal with transcendence. All these schools, however, claim to reject pantheism. Bacon is also not a metaphysician in the classical Western sense. He, however, does not see the immanent or reductionist material. For him, nature, as we know it, is not enough. In mystical language, one could say that it was necessary to journey from external and apparent reality to the internal and substantial, discovering the womb of the world and the primordial seed. It would be necessary to go deeper into the immanent to overcome it with the discovery of the absolute that transcends it. On the whole of knowledge contained in nature, Bacon writes the following words:

> Let no one expect great progress in the sciences, especially on their practical side, until natural philosophy is brought to the particular sciences and the particular sciences are incorporated into natural philosophy. Because they are dependent on it, astronomy, optics, music, innumerable mechanical arts, medicine itself, and, what is astonishing, natural and political philosophy and the logical sciences have not reached any depth, but only glide across the surface and variety of things.[80]

Paracelsus, according to Japiassu (1934-2015), presented to the world mystical medicine or the elements of alchemy in the Christian

---

[79] Ascetic practice present in the Orthodox Church.
[80] BACON, Francis. *Novum Organum* [1620], p. 48.

mysticism of Meister Eckhart (1260-1328).[81] The resemblance to Bacon comes into play when Japiassu discusses the nature of life in Paracelsian research. Like Paracelsus, Bacon did not separate nature from a "living" reality that was hidden from human eyes, a substance, truth itself—life itself in the full sense—must be discovered by method. In this sense, Bacon continued the project of Paracelsus and Roger Bacon to unite knowledge hitherto veiled in nature, in order to lead man and the world to progress.[82] Knowing what Paracelsus and the alchemists thought about Mercury, Sulfur, and Salt—Paracelsus saw them as a sort of triad—Lord Verulam gave some continuity to the validation of these elements. In his own words: "There are two great families of things [...] Mercury and Sulfur [...] (for Sal, which is the third principle, is a compound of the other two) [...] flammable, and non-flammable; mature and crude; oily and liquid."[83] Cintas highlights the fact that,

> Bacon mentions the term vitriol oil, common among alchemists, which is generally agreed to be sulfuric acid. He also used the rhetorical name of sulfur oil presumably to denote the same substance.

Cintas continues: "However, in his subsequent work on the *History of Density and Rarity*, which is a collection of observations within the third part of the Great Initiation, Bacon listed the two oils separately and with different densities." Finally, "Similarly, he freely used the Latin terms *aqua fortis* (nitric acid) and royal water [...] (nitric acid: hydrochloric acid) without a clear distinction between them."[84]

In dealing with Giordano Bruno (1548-1600), Japiassu denies that he was a martyr of science – at least of the 'science' known to

---

[81] JAPIASSU, Hilton. *The Hidden Face of Modern Science*. Rio de Janeiro: Imago Publishing House, 2013, p. 320.

[82] For information on Paracelsus and Roger Bacon see Ibidem, p. 324.

[83] BACON, Francis. *The Works of Francis Bacon, Lord Chancellor of England*. Philadelphia: Edited by Basil Montagu, Carey and Hart, 1844, p. 53.

[84] CINTAS, Pedro. *Francis Bacon: An Alchemical Odyssey Through Novum Organum*. Bull. Hist. Chem., VOLUME 28, Number 2, 2003, USA, p. 68.

modernity.[85] The Brunian idea of the infinite universe, its mysticism, and the interpretation it gave of Copernican heliocentrism, making analogies between itself and the old solar cults, clearly denote to Japiassu that Bruno does not fit the scientific model that has crystallized in modernity, but rather the mystical model of science of the ancient world which was on the rise.[86] Tomasio Campanella had also linked knowledge to this. In *The City of the Sun*, he is optimistic about the advances that knowledge could bring to a new world, a republic of sages, in which the inequalities of the present world would be overcome.[87] Nicholas of Cusa, with the theme of the reflection of God in reality, also discusses infinity and its relation to the cosmos. Pico della Mirandola taught that men, possessed of free will, could ascend from mere creatures to become connoisseurs of reality and dominate nature. Ficino, in turn, continues the Renaissance and Neoplatonic thinking of man as a microcosm that seeks to know the infinite in the macrocosm (the universe). This spirit that unites men like Agrippa, Bruno, Campanella, Cusa, Mirandola, and Ficino, in one way or another, was influenced by Platonism and especially by Neoplatonism, whose most famous exponent is Plotinus (205-270). Their thoughts had notable similarities to the Baconian concepts of truth, nature, knowledge, and progress. It is also worth remembering that Platonic dualistic thinking was not retained by all his disciples and that much of Platonism or Neoplatonism identifies the cosmos with monism. The relationship between Neoplatonists and Stoicism may, according to scholars, be one of the causes of this change. Plotinus, for example, is known as a monist. The critique of Platonic apriorism would, therefore, be best described as a critique of its dualistic system, which had excluded Neoplatonic monism as deserving of exactly the same criticism that Bacon had for Plato.

Renaissance thinking, influenced by Neoplatonism, although it was susceptible to the criticism of Baconian thought, clearly used ideas and presuppositions common to Bacon, which makes Japiassu and the other authors mentioned here consistent in their arguments

---

[85] See JAPIASSU, Hilton. *The Hidden Face of Modern Science*, p. 100.
[86] Ibid., p. 100.
[87] Ibid., p. 104.

connecting Bacon with the mysticism of the Renaissance, a mysticism which, as affirmed by Japiassu, was not only present in men of science like Bacon, but also in other great scientists, such as Kepler (1571-1630), and Newton (1642-1727). Yet, the fact that Bacon introduced himself as a radical empiricist is not compatible with his notion that nature retained the idea of the divine. And this was not unusual at the time of experimentation in which he had lived. As he wrote, "[that] natural philosophy be brought to the particular sciences, and the particular sciences be incorporated into natural philosophy [!]"[88] This, for him, means: "every atom should be studied as a sphere that composes the absolute." The idea of wholeness, of a liberating totality, as seen in *New Atlantis*, guided scientific aspiration. The study of particular things was taken so seriously by him that it must be said that the investigation of each particle would have universal implications and that the totalizing aspect would be in each particle as if the infinite were "finite" and the finite "infinite" – if these neologisms are permissible here. With this, the "limits" of inherited sin would be overcome, since "limitation" itself would be made accessible to men by science. This, after reaching the totality of Natural Philosophy, would render omnipotence. Or rather, the deity itself would be a scientist.

2.5.1 RHETORIC, CONSPIRACY, AND MAGIC

Some authors have delved into conspirology with Bacon. They believe that the real author of Shakespeare's plays (1564-1616) was Lord Verulam. *Bacon, Shakespeare and the Rosicrucians*, for example, argues that "[the plays] of Shakespeare contain evidence of ancient Hermetic sources and mystery – Rosicrucian or of Masonic origin."[89] Miller notes that "The most complete work on Bacon's Promus [of Formularies and Elagancies] was made by Pott in 1883, who attempted to prove the connection between Promus and Shakespeare's plays."[90]

---

[88] BACON, Francis. *Novum Organum* [1620], Paragraph lxx.
[89] WIGSTON, W. F. C. *Bacon, Shakespeare and the Rosicrucians*, p. xix.
[90] MILLER, Kevin. *The Commonplace Book: The Key to Sir Francis Bacon's Philosophy and Method*. Kansas: Thesis Presented to the Faculty of the Department

Besides the negative idea that Shakespeare did not possess the necessary intellectual gifts for his famous literary endeavor, this also involves the idea that Bacon, as a man of science and politics, would prevent himself from being exposed as a man of poetry and theater. There are, however, sophisticated arguments for this:

1. Baconian rhetoric and the rhetoric of Shakespeare's characters demonstrate suggestive similarities;
2. Bacon using the poetic genre of the theater, and the use of pseudonyms would not be strange for him. On the contrary, if the thesis that he secretly wrote as a Rosicrucian was accepted, this was a common practice;
3. Bacon showed excellence in the writing of prose and poetry when analyzing the ancient myths;
4. Shakespeare's writings have relevant evidence of the author's knowledge of mysticism.

Some of the authors who see good reasons for defending Bacon's authorship of Shakespeare's works are found in the *Francis Bacon Society* and quoted among the writers of the *Baconian* periodical, namely Andrew Lily, Michael Buhagiar, T. D. Bokeham, James Loren, N. D. Van Edmund. Other authors include the American writer Delia Bacon (1811-1859)—it is said that the editor of Bacon's works, John Spedding (1808-1881), knowing of Delia's thesis, came to be in doubt about this possibility—Richard Allan Wagner, and the famous American historian James Phinney Baxter (1831-1921).[91] Regarding this, the Rosicrucian writings were full of poetry. There is also a suggestion that Bacon's *New Atlantis* exerted an influence on John Heydon's *Voyage to the Land of the Rosicrucians*, and also that the English mystic Robert Fludd (1574-1637) was aware of the Baconian use of theater to convey the teachings of the mystery school, as he had written respectfully for the Rosicrucians of Frankfurt, in Germany.[92]

---

of English Kansas State Teachers College, 1968, p. 81.

[91] See BAXTER, James. *The Greatest of Literary Problems, the Authorship of the Shakespeare Works; an Exposition of all the Points at Issue, from their Inception to the Present Moment.* London: Forgotten Books, 2015.

[92] The controversial writer goes so far as to say that Heydon plagiarized the

Baxter suggests, along with Wigston, through an analysis of the Shakespearean character Sly, the work *Megera Domada*, can be used to demonstrate the antagonism between the real Shakespeare and Bacon.

The purpose of this work is not to defend Bacon's authorship of Shakespeare's works, however. The inclusion of this subsection is due to the presence of this possibility, based on research in the academic environment, which strengthens the evidence for the presence of the Hermetic thought in Bacon, as well as its association with the secret transmission of his thoughts.[93]

2.6 Baconian Mysticism and Aristotle: Asymmetries & Possible Confluences

It is important to address Bacon's criticism of Aristotle in light of the mystical assumptions that surround the English philosopher. To investigate the real dimension of this importance, Aristotelian thought will be divided into metaphysics, epistemology, physics, and ethics. In turn, investigations will be made on the presence of mysticism in Bacon's criticism of each of these spheres of Aristotle's thought. The intention, however, is not to make an exhaustive analysis of the Aristotelian ideas, since this work is dedicated to the study of Bacon and not Aristotle. However, the ideas of the Greek philosopher studied gradually in each sphere proposed here, will be presented in a succinct way and without great pretensions.

New Atlantis of Bacon for his Rosicrucian treatise. See WEBSTER, Nestar. *Secret Societies and Subversive Movements*. London: Eworld Inc., 2014.

[93] Among other famous mystics who were in contact with England during the sixteenth century are Edward Kelley (1555-1597) and John Dee (1527-1608).

2.6.1 BACONIAN MYSTICISM: ARISTOTELIAN METAPHYSICS & EPISTEMOLOGY

Unlike Plato,[94] Aristotle does not have a "world of ideas." He was a hymnologist, and he believed that things were composed of form and matter. For it, nothing comes to mind without first having passed through the senses. In this way, it gives greater prominence to the induction than Plato, who emphasizes the importance of mathematics and geometric forms. However, like Plato, Aristotle was metaphysical. Aksoy says that,

> for Aristotle, philosophy, empirical sciences, and ethics has a common ground, namely, metaphysics. According to Aristotle, metaphysics, as the first philosophy, could be established through a certain intuition about the world.[95]

Aksoy goes on to state: "Bacon, however, excludes this kind of knowledge (that is, a knowledge that can be reached from a reason that is largely in the objective world) of the field of knowledge."[96]

His metaphysics, however, was different from that of Platonism, which was bound up with dualism, the idea of the fall of the soul, and the doctrine of the world of ideas. For Aristotle, being is the Immobile Motor that causes movement, the Pure Act, which has no need to be potentially anything else.[97] This Being, however, is not an *ex nihilo* Creator, as in Christianity. He constitutes the world, but he is not a personal being who intervenes in the world performing miracles, as in the theist model known in the West. Christianity, especially Thomas Aquinas (1225-1274), "Christianized" Aristotle in order to make his thinking compatible with the theistic model of a

---

[94] Plato will sometimes be quoted in the following sections because he is an important author both to understand Bacon's criticism and to Aristotle's thought, who was to some extent his disciple.

[95] AKSOY, Ilgin. *Francis Bacon on the Question of the Knowledge*. Istanbul: Thesis presented to Istanbul Bilgi University, 2013, p. 16.

[96] Ibid., p. 16.

[97] See ARISTOTLE. *Metaphysics (I and II)*. Trad. Marcelo Perine, from the Italian version of Giovanni Reale. São Paulo: Loyola, 2002.

personal God and with the doctrine of the Creator *ex nihilo*. Jewish and Islamic thinkers have similarly used Aristotelian philosophy within their respective traditions, such as the Jewish Maimonides (1135-1204) and the Muslim Averroes (1126-1198), by way of example. The fact that a good number of modern scholars dealing with questions about the scientific method have separated it from classical metaphysics and theism does not mean that they have been inflected to mystical influences. If, on the one hand, the Gnosticism of the first centuries of Christianity had been influenced by dualism, and St. Augustine had synthesized the Platonic dualism in Christianity, the monist model of Neoplatonism influenced by Stoicism, Plotinus' monism and Renaissance Neoplatonism have in common with Aristotle the absence of a recourse to the ontological abyss between the transcendent and the immanent to explain metaphysics.

This too, Bacon has in common with Aristotle.[98] According to Weeks, as has been said earlier, Bacon's investigation of the Cupid myth reveals Bacon's own cosmology, whose origin would be the original chaos. If Weeks is correct, Bacon's cosmology is closer to the Greeks—which includes Aristotle himself—than to Augustinian and Thomistic Christianity. Bacon himself considered the pre-Socratic atomist Democritus (460-370 BC) superior to Plato and Aristotle.

Aristotle addresses God from a fundamentally speculative bias, so he does not properly deal with the Greek deities. In Bacon's context, on the other hand, the political centrality of religion greatly hindered the rational treatment of divinity without direct implications for

---

[98] Aristotle believes it is possible to study the immanent and the moving: "[1025b 18] Since the science of nature is also circumscribed to a genus of being (for it is limited to the kind of essence in which the principle of motion and rest it is evident that it is neither practical science nor productive science (for the principle of what is susceptible of being produced is in the producer of intelligence, or technique, or some capacity), and the principle of what is susceptible of being done is in the agent (the choice; in fact, the same thing is susceptible to choice and susceptible of being made); consequently, if all rational knowledge is either practical, or productive, or theoretical, the science of nature is to be theoretical, but theoretical about such an entity that it is capable of moving, and only about the kind of essence that conforms to the definition more often than not, and which is not separate." ARISTOTELE. *Metaphysics - Book VI*. Trad. br. Lucas Angioni. Campinas: IFCH-UNICAMP, 2007, 1025b 18.

the practical life of the religious people. It is possible that Bacon preferred a less controversial technique: to prevent metaphysics from gaining a status equal to that of physics in order to guarantee the philosopher's freedom from religion. Hence, the Baconian view that faith should not mix with science. It was not that Bacon did not believe in religion, rather he wanted to prevent religion, which had dominated the studies of metaphysics during the Middle Ages, from interfering with his work. However, what is argued here is that, even if it bequeaths to metaphysics a lower place in the scale of knowledge, below the knowledge acquired by its inductive method, Bacon continued with assumptions that are structurally metaphysical. What were these metaphysical assumptions?

1. Bacon believed that the inductive method would lead man to the knowledge of the truth.
2. He also believed that the knowledge of the truth in nature would lead man to progress – freeing man from the social ills arising from Original Sin.
3. All this, however, would only be possible, he said, if the correct inductive method were applied.

However, it is necessary to ask: if it is the method that provides the sure knowledge of reality, how can it be predicted where it will lead the world? Such a statement would only be consistent with Baconian reasoning if it arose from the application of the method. Thus, by this logic, the legitimation of the method escapes the criterion that Bacon points out, and it must be acknowledged that the criticism of Aristotle, especially those who accuse the Stagirite of perverting the inductive method with undue anticipations, could be applied to him even though it would be difficult to admit that Bacon's notion of first philosophy, that is, the notion of an absolute science, was possible only by reference to method. This issue may warrant another consideration. Now Bacon had a notion of knowledge or gnosis that was not removed from empiricism. Baconian progress is the real union between knowing and being, that is, between knowledge (gnosis) and truth. In fact, Bacon postulates that scientific method will inevitably lead society to progress, that is, teleologically.[99] When there was a real dominion of nature by man through the inductive method, the evils acquired by inadequacy between the cosmos and man would be overcome, so that man would attain knowledge of the cosmos and evolve in relation to his past, knowing not only the present and the future, but also the past, in order to solve the gaps left behind. This, however, also needs a metaphysical foundation to be deduced, since such a notion exists in Bacon before the inductive method is put into practice over the whole cosmos. Contrary to Aristotle, therefore, Bacon does not pose as an expert in metaphysics, although he has theorized about it, as seen in *The Advancement of Learning*. Also, unlike Aristotle, Bacon did not base it on a deductive logic in the formal sense, nor see metaphysical reasons for it. When Bacon criticized the Aristotelian anticipations of knowledge, that is, his deductive presuppositions, which could be considered as presuppositions based on metaphysics, it is not that Bacon had no presupposition whatsoever or that he had no metaphysical notion at all, but rather that Bacon's metaphysical presuppositions were close to the mystic monism of the Renaissance, and not to classical Aristotelian metaphysics.[100]

The theory of causes—formal, material, efficient, and final—would be partly correct, for Bacon. For the true inductivist, it would be necessary to stick to the form and matter of the thing and not to speculate about its purpose or efficient cause on the same level of formal and material causes. The study of form and matter is performed so that, in his view, one could ultimately arrive at the answers that Aristotle wanted to anticipate. It is not that Bacon had no metaphysical presuppositions, but that he followed a method

---

[99] According to Couliano, the teleological optimism of the mystics of Bacon's era was significant: "The editors of the Rosicrucian manifestos [...] date to the death of Christian Rosenkreuz in 1484 and the date of the discovery of his tomb in 1604, representing the exact interval between two great conjunctions [...] the dates coincided perfectly with the astrological date and a new world was expected after 1604. The spreading of the secret order founded Christian Rosenkreuz could only satisfy even more the hope aroused by the event whose importance was emphasized by Kepler." COULIANO, Ioan. *Eros and Magic in Renaissance*. Translated to english by Margaret Cook. London: University Chicago Press, 1987, pp. 185-186.

[100] BACON, Francis. *The Advancement of Learning* [1605], p. 140.

whereby the rigid study of material nature would lead him to absolute truth. Such an absolute could not be limited to the initial concept that the researcher had of matter. In this sense, there is a transcendence by immanence in Bacon, and the pursuit of philosophy first in the whole of nature. According to his own words:

> It is therefore expedient, before establishing the distributions ... [of true knowledge] ... to establish and constitute a universal [or absolute] science, which, under the name of *Philosophia Prima*, primitive or supreme philosophy, is like the way main or common that there are before the paths divide and separate.[101]

The knowledge of forms, for Aristotle,[102] is the knowledge of things themselves, in their formal-material reality.[103] Aristotle presents himself as less distant from "materialism" than from Platonic "dualism."[104] The problem is that the method he used could not be accepted by Renaissance Neoplatonism. According to Aksoy,

> Aristotle proposed specific axioms for various scientific disciplines; he lacked in his thought the proposal of a dominant principle for all science. This lack also existed the contemporary science of Bacon, according to this one. The dominant principle in question is what can be called a methodology.[105]

Some of the Aristotelian assumptions that could not be reconciled with the Renaissance mystics are: 1) the idea that it was possible to reduce gnosis to a linguistic knowledge of a material thing. For

---

[101] Ibid., p. 136.

[102] Aristotle. *Animated Presentation*, translation and notes by Maria Cecília Gomes dos Reis. Sao Paulo: Ed. 34, 2006.

[103] According to the popular or vulgar interpretation of his thought.

[104] The Aristotelian theory of knowledge is more "sensory." "All men have by nature the desire to know: a proof of this is the pleasure of sensations, for even out of their utility they please us by themselves and more than all visuals." ARISTOTLE, *Metaphysics*. Translation and Localization Vizenzo Cocco. São Paulo: Abril S. A. Cultural, 1984, p. 6.

[105] AKSOY, Ilgin. *Francis Bacon on the Question of the Knowledge*, p. 19.

example, many understand that his view of the world made him believe that the material thing was exactly the same as the linguistic idea of the thing, that is, he believed in the correctness of the correspondence between language and things. If one can accuse Plato of separating too much form, one can accuse Aristotle of not knowing how to separate form correctly. If it were asked "what would a stone be if the name "stone" was not given to it", that is, what would this thing be without its name, Aristotle would have to recognize that to know the thing called "stone" it would take more than reason and logic, both use of language, but intuition or mystical illumination of the thing itself and for itself, which transcends language. That would be gnosis to the mystics. 2) Aristotelian logic does not credit due importance to supralinguistic intuition, that is, the "knowledge-gnosis" transmitted by logos-logic should, for mystics, be beyond the syntactic-semantic content of the three principles of logic. In other words, the knowledge that is transmitted by the three principles of logic is not in itself false, but according to the mystics there is more than one linguistic way of transmitting the *logos* – even though the logos itself is the same. In Aristotle, therefore, there would not be a problem with logic itself, but regarding the linguistic reduction made in the transmission of it. For example, the principle of identity is in the sentence of Parmenides (530-460 BC) is it "the Being is" or the absolute Being itself, which is transmitted by the sentence "identity is a principle of logic?" The mystics understood that there were varied linguistic ways of speaking of the same supralinguistically intuited truth. The Baconian inductive method sees dialectics, logic, and language as potentially limiting knowledge.

Gloarke states that "Aristotelian emphasis on science does not eliminate the need for direct mental enlightenment as a source of knowledge."[106] He continues,

> If, however, *noesis* is the experience of the enlightened being, it is also an instance of inductive reasoning ... because it requires a movement from the particular to the universal. Beginning with

---

[106] GROARKE, Louis. *An Aristotelian Account of Induction: Creating Something from Nothing*. Ontario: McGill-Queen's University Press, 2009, p. 283.

ideas of particular things, one arrives, finally, at the knowledge of the most universal ideas.[107]

Besides that: Bacon preferred inductive logic to deductive logic. Understood in this Platonic sense, the noun, which denotes the activity of pure thought or intelligent understanding, represents a form of immediate enlightenment that provides direct access to forms. As we see in the split-line analogy, noesis transcends language. In this final phase of knowledge, [*The Republic*, book 6] "the soul leaves the hypotheses and arrives at a principle that is above the hypotheses, not making use of images [...] but proceeding only in and through the own ideas". Plato thus places the greatest form of knowledge in a kind of immediate illumination without words. He places dialectic or διάλεκτος (*dialektos*) at the service of inspiration, not inspiration at the service of dialectic.[108]

However, his rejection of the Aristotelian deduction was due not to the fact that Aristotle had used deductive logic against inductive logic in all cases, since Bacon knew that Aristotle was also an inductor, because aiming towards *The Great Instauration*,[109] Bacon wanted to reach the full knowledge of the cosmos, synthesizing everything in mathematical language, and knew, along with many of his contemporaries, that the way Aristotle used logic prevented an epistemology from developing into knowledge of the thing itself and for itself. For Bacon, true knowledge, the knowledge that reaches the hidden thing, behind the linguistic prejudices, must follow a method different from the Aristotelian method. For Bacon, the Aristotelian dialectic prejudiced the empirical, making it, therefore, invalid:

> Aristotle [...] corrupted with his dialectic the natural philosophy: in forming the world on the basis of the categories; by attributing to the human soul, the noblest of substances, a genre extracted from the second concepts; in dealing with the question of density and rarefaction, which indicates whether bodies occupy more or less extensions, according to their dimensions, by means of

---

[107] Ibid., p. 290.

[108] Ibid., p. 290.

[109] The *Novum Organum* work was written as part of *The Great Instauration*.

the cold distinction of power and act; by conferring upon each body only its own motion, stating that if the body participates in another movement, it comes from an external cause; by imposing upon the nature of things innumerable arbitrary distinctions, and being ever more solicitous in formulating answers and presenting something positive in words than the intimate truth of things.[110]

Thus, it inferred that not only the similarity of his critique to Aristotelian epistemology but also his appreciation of new logic perpetrated by Pedro Ramo.[111]

2.6.2 BACONIAN MYSTICISM: ARISTOTELIAN PHYSICS & ETHICS

Unlike Plato, who saw the physical (material) world as devoid of ontological consistency, Aristotle saw the physical world as inseparable from forms.[112] Movement, as matter, was not knowable in Plato. But this cannot be said to the same for Aristotle since, in his view, the eternal and the temporal could be understood. He developed studies on the function of the four elements (water, earth, fire, and air) and quintessence (ether), in rectilinear motion brought

---

[110] BACON, Francis. *Novum Organum* [1620], p. 32.

[111] Still on the dialectic, Bacon says: "Someone else may, perhaps, invoke the help of the dialectic, which in name only has relation with what it proposes. Indeed, the invention of the dialectic does not refer to the fundamental principles and axioms that underpin the arts [...] And when, surrounded by the most curious and importunate, it is interpreted in relation to the proofs and the discovery of the first principles and axioms, dialectic repulses them with the already well-known answer, referring them to the faith and oath that must be given to the principles of each of the arts." Ibid., p. 50.

[112] Since the science of nature studies magnitudes, motion, and time, and each of these is by necessity or infinite or finite, although not every thing is either infinite or finite (as for example a condition or a point, since it is not necessary that these things have to be either infinite or finite), then it will be convenient for anyone who deals with nature to investigate whether the infinite is or is not; and, if it is, what it is. One sign that research on the infinite belongs to this science is in the fact that all those who seem to have dealt worthily with this part of philosophy have spoken of the infinite and have all understood it as a beginning of things. See ARISTOTLE. *Physics*. Madrid: Editorial Gredos, 1985, pp. 187-188.

about by forces – gravitational force down and up, vacuum, and the circular motion of celestial bodies etc. Aristotle's physics dominated the Western physics model.[113] In the Middle Ages, however, it had been attacked by Christian and Muslim intellectuals. Considerations such as the one Aristotle made about movement, stating that a constant force leads to a uniform movement, no longer possessed the influence that they had been accorded in the distant past. Scholars challenged him: acceleration would imply nonuniform motion since the present velocity was distinct from the initial velocity, and doubted the Aristotelian notion that there would be infinite speed in the vacuum. When Galileo's experience in Pisa became famous—after having already studied the fall of objects in a dense element, water—he discredited the Aristotelian thesis that objects with different weights fell at different times, Bacon was already in the final moments of his life.

Nevertheless, Bacon could contemplate all the repercussions of the famous critic Copernicus to the geocentric model of world, which had been defended by Aristotle. Also, peculiar positions, such as Giordano Bruno's[114] idea of the infinity of worlds, and the relationships made between infinity and cosmos by Nicholas of Cusa,[115] were publicly acknowledged as anti-Aristotelian in Bacon's time. Thus, Bacon's criticism of Aristotle's physics occurs in the wake of the progressive spirit of his time, in which the figure of the scholastic tradition, Aristotle, had to give way to a new investigation of the cosmos. Bacon did not agree with the way Aristotle divided the cosmos: Aristotle saw in the sublunary world one inferior to the lunar world, in such a way that, for example, he believed that the surface of the moon was smooth. Bacon, nevertheless, showed himself to be knowledgeable on ideas of the star as fire and the pyramidal form of the flame, analyzing them critically, but without

---

[113] ARISTOTLE. *Physics I and II*. Preface, translation, introduction and comments: Lucas Angioni. Campinas: Publisher of Unicamp. 2009.

[114] White claims there is some influence of Giordano Bruno on Bacon. See STRAUSS. Leo; CROPSEY, Joseph. *History of Political Philosophy*. Francis Bacon Section, p. 370.

[115] See CUSA, Nicholas. *The Learned Ignorance*. Trad. br. Reinholdo Aluysio Ullman. Edipcurs, 2002.

bias. It is interesting to note that in the *History of Life and Death*, after defining the spirits as lifeless spirits (living bodies) and living spirits (of animate bodies), the English philosopher said that the former is of the same substance of air, and the second as the same substance of the flame (fire).[116] He even went so far as to say: "Whatever may be repaired without it's whole being destroyed is, like the vestal fire, potentially eternal."[117] He also opposed the Aristotelian concept of incorruptibility of the cosmos, notwithstanding, in the book *Descriptio Globi Intellectualis*, to emphasize Venus and Mercury as satellites of the sun,[118] as was done in Egyptian astrology, to discuss the growth of flame and brightness in the region next to Venus[119] and to define circles as "perfect."

Bacon still rejected the way Aristotle undertook induction. Baconian induction, as a tool of the *Great Instauration* project, placed importance on mathematical knowledge not shared by Aristotle, who criticized Plato's use of mathematics, and who was less apprehensive than Lord Verulam – Grant, was an opportunist in pointing this out.[120] For Bacon, the Stagirite added to the induction speculations which were not compatible with empirical observation and made anticipations to the inductive method, which rendered it unsuccessful and made his entire physics project accountable. He understood that the Aristotelian distinction between the act and power impaired his philosophy. Contrary to what Aristotle thought, he understood that the "law of the act" is movement. The idea of Pure Act would be a preconceived—and even an unnecessary idea—for the use of method:

---

[116] See ZATERKA, Luciana. *Francis Bacon and the Question of Human Longevity*. Scientiæ Zudia, São Paulo, v. 13, n. 3, 2015, pp. 495-517.

[117] BACON, Francis. *The Works of Francis Bacon Vol. 5: Translations of the Philosophical Works 2*. Edited by Spedding, Ellis, Heath. New York: Cambridge University Press, 2011, pp. 218, 322-330.

[118] BACON, Francis. *The Philosophical Works of Francis Bacon - Descriptio Globi Intellectualis*. Routledge, New York, 2011, p. 684.

[119] See BACON, Francis. *The Philosophical Works of Francis Bacon - Thema Coeli*. New York: Routledge, 2011, p. 704.

[120] See GRANT, Edward. *A History of Natural Philosophy: From the Ancient World to the Nineteenth Century*. New York: Cambridge University Press, 2007, p. 308.

> But it is better to divide into parts the nature than to translate them into abstractions. Thus proceeded the school of Democritus, who more than others penetrated the secrets of nature. What must be considered above all is matter, its *schematisms, metaesquematisms, the pure act,* and the *law of the act,* which is the movement.[121]

Bacon did not yet conceive of forms as entities dissociated from material things:

> The form of a given nature is such that, once established, nature follows unfailingly. It is present whenever this nature is also universally affirmed and constantly inherent in it. And the same form is such that, if it departs, nature unfailingly vanishes; that whenever he is absent, nature is absent, when he wholly denies it, because it alone is present in it.[122]

The whole of the Baconian critique of Aristotle was, however, not due to a need to return to Platonic "dualism," but to deepen the monism which Aristotle's Neoplatonists and Immanenism ("materialism") approached, but for various reasons failed to develop fully.

Even if the attack on the method calls into question all of Aristotle's conclusions, Bacon once again shared some Aristotelian assumptions present in Neoplatonism and Hermeticism and continued with the mystical spirit of the Renaissance. Some Baconian assumptions, in the wake of this spirit, led him to:

1. Separate revealed theology from philosophy;
2. Prefer empiricist monism to theoretical dualism;
3. Reject Aristotelian concepts about the physical world, such as the supremacy of the lunar sphere over the sublunary and the incorruptibility of the cosmos, not because it rejected an empiric monist view of the world, but because Aristotle did

---

[121] BACON, Francis. *Novum Organum* [1620], p. 32.
[122] Ibid., pp. 95-96.

not know how to develop empirically, being unable to reach the knowledge of reality;

4. Believe, as non-dualistic, that the knowledge of forms and the knowledge of physics are interconnected. Aristotle, for him, was not wrong about this, but on the way to know the forms;

5. Understand that Aristotelian physics must be overcome not by a religious theory, by a mechanical rationality, by dualism, or by an atheist empire, but by an empire that leads to the absolute which is hidden, absolute, and when it is known, will satisfy both the desires of science and those of religion.

Aristotelian ethics, like Plato's ethics, were the ethics of virtue. Plato affirmed that there are four cardinal virtues: prudence, justice, fortitude, and temperance. For Aristotle, the study and practice of ethics were aimed at leading man to the common good. Man is a political animal, for Aristotle. Therefore, it is social in nature. But every man seeks happiness. This is the Aristotelian doctrine of *eudaimonia*. When, however, individual happiness is guided by selfishness and leads to the unhappiness of others, one is acting in an unethical way.[123] The ethical man, on the contrary, must recognize that individual happiness only materializes in collective happiness. In this way, action that is ethical always aims at the common good.

---

[123] "But since there are many acts, arts and sciences, many are also their ends: the end of medical art is health, shipbuilding is a ship, that of strategy is victory, and that of economy is wealth. But when such arts are subordinated to a single faculty—just as the saddlery and other arts dealing with horse dressing are included in the art of riding, and this, along with all military actions, in strategy, there are other arts which are also included in thirds—in all of them the ends of the fundamental arts should be preferred for all subordinate purposes, because the latter are sought for the good of the former. It makes no difference whether the ends of the actions are the activities themselves or something distinct from them, as is the case with the sciences just mentioned [...] [Happiness is] always sought by itself and never seen in anything else, we have chosen them in the interest of happiness, thinking that their possession will make us happy [...] And the things that tend to produce virtue considered as a whole are those acts prescribed by law for the purpose of education for the common good." ARISTOTLE. *Ethics to Nicomachus*. Trad. br. Leonel Vallandro Nicolasch. 2.ed São Paulo: New Cultural, 1991, pp. 3, 10, 10.

The ethical man is also a wise man, who uses *phronesis*, since ethics are, according to Aristotle, the wisdom and practical use of this wisdom in ethical action.[124] Bacon understood, in turn, that a theory about ethics cannot precede knowledge of facts. For him, the danger of imposing speculation on reality should lead the scientist to be cautious about the theorizing of ethics. That is distinct from Aristotle. On the other hand, Bacon also possessed certain moral presuppositions. He believed that a just government (a position which sets him in opposition to that of the later French Revolution on religion, even though some French revolutionaries praised Bacon) believed that science had a duty to favor society and to lead it towards progress:

> As long as this is within the reach of my pen, to settle a sociable intercourse between Antiquity and progress, it seems to me better to follow that path than to the altars, that is, where it is possible without lacking in superior obligations, and therefore, to preserve the ancient terms, although at times it changes its uses and definitions in accordance with the moderate power of civil government, where, although there is some change, this is fulfilled which Tacitus wisely points out: *Eadem magistratuum vocabula*.[125]

In addition to this, he related his work as a scientist to a prophetic mission, whose reach for knowledge-gnosis would lead men to free themselves from deception.

These assumptions did not make him follow Aristotle's ethics, but he shared with the Stagirite the notion that certain principles—though in Bacon were not clear—should guide professional activity, which includes the work of the scientist. But, were these moral assumptions of Bacon possible, with him being so radically inductive? The answer lies in the fact that Bacon accepted certain "intuitive" truths of the Hermetic era that surrounded him. For him,

---

[124] ARISTOTLE. *Ethics to Nicomachus*. Second ed. Translation, additional texts, and notes. Bauru: EDIPRO, 2007.

[125] BACON, Francis. *The Advancement of Learning* [1605], p. 145.

knowledge-gnosis was an intrinsic necessity of man, the unveiling of the hidden truth in nature, his mission, and the progress brought to society by the enlightened scientist, was his glory.[126] This was accompanied by religious bias in Bacon's thought.

---

[126] Unlike "conventional" Gnostics, who were pessimistic about the "demiurgical" world, elevating the glory of the spiritual world, Bacon believed in science as the source of a purity similar to that which the Gnostics believed to be the spirit or the soul. The glory of science, then, would be to make the world "pure." Matter and spirit, cosmos and purity, would be united by science. Hence, Bacon's closeness to monism is greater than with the dualism of these Gnostics.

3.

THE INFLUENCE OF PROTESTANT CHRISTIANITY ON BACON'S THOUGHT

In order to undertake a critical inquiry into the influence of Protestant Christianity on Bacon's thought, this chapter will be divided into seven sections. The first will introduce the context of Protestant religiosity in Bacon's time. The second section will study the influence of Puritan Protestantism on Bacon, delimiting the differences and similarities between him and the English philosopher. The third is intended to reflect on Bacon's epistemological doctrine and its concept of method and religion. The fourth section will investigate the relationship between theology and science for Bacon, or, more precisely, the theologization of science that occurs in his thinking. The fifth will provide continuity to the theme of the previous section, emphasizing the eschatological doctrine present in the English philosopher, in addition to explaining Bacon's criticism of Roman Catholic Christianity, that is, Christianity in the medieval West. The sixth section will provide a comparative table to summarize the extent of religion's influence on Bacon. The final section will condense theses developed in the previous sections and investigate the extent of their influence on the view that Bacon held of ancient philosophers—especially Plato and Aristotle—including the possibility of the existence of prejudices in Bacon's evaluation and criticism of these authors.

3.1 Preliminary Questions

Against the background of humanism and rebirth, in addition to the debilitation that the struggle against the advance of the Ottoman Turks caused to the Catholic Church, the Protestant Reformation established itself. It is one of the causes of the passage from the Middle Ages to the modern world. The separation of England from the papacy came with controversy. King Henry VIII (1491-1547), who was famous for being a womanizer, wanted to separate from his wife, Catherine of Aragon (1483-1536). Their marriage sealed a political agreement between England and Catholic Spain, and because the Catholic Church did not accept divorce and remarriage, the Pope refused the request for divorce made by the king of England. Henry VIII, taking advantage of this contrariety, declared himself supreme head of the Church of England, untying the table of the Roman See.[127] In principle, the Church of England remained Catholic. There was, however, a significant body of men with Protestant ideas in the region who were striving to promote reform in the Church. Even though Mary Stuart (1542-1587), reconnected England to the Roman See, which was later undone, she gradually became distant from typical Roman practices.[128] While adhering to many postulates of the Protestant faith, especially under the reigns of Edward VI (1537-1553), Elizabeth (1533-1603), and James I (1566-1625), the most radical groups of the British Reformation were dissatisfied with the direction of the Church of England. To them, it had not fully reformed. It was then necessary to complete the reform of the Church.[129] Levellers, one of the separatist groups, called for greater

---

[127] See FOXE, John. *Book of Martyrs*. Trad. br. Almiro Pisetta. São Paulo: Christian World, 2005, pp. 123-273.

[128] See Ibid., pp. 123-273.

[129] "The revolt within the Revolution [...] has taken many forms, some of which are better known than others. Groups such as levellers, diggers and pentamonarchists have offered new political solutions (and in the case of diggers, also new economic solutions). The various sects—Baptists, Quakers, Muggletonians—proposed new religious solutions. Other groups have formulated skeptical questions about all the institutions and beliefs of their society – seekers, ranters, once again the diggers." HILL, Christopher. *The World at its Head: Radical Ideas During the English Revolution of 1640*. Trad. br. Renato Janine Ribeiro. São

equality of goods among the population. The Christian church, they understood, should be the ambassador of this equality, the driving force of the awakening of humanity to the need for the common good. Richard Overton (1599-1664), was a prominent leader who promoted a more materialistic Christian worldview and defended the end of the English monarchist system.[130] Gerrard Winstanley (1609-1676), one of those dissatisfied with the established church, preached a more radical message than the Levellers. For him, original sin is linked to private property. Regeneration occurs when everyone lives, as brothers, communally. The message was a kind of Christian communism.[131] Those who shared their ideas, the diggers, divided up all goods among themselves in rural communities, and claimed to be restoring early Christianity, going back to a practice from the time of the apostles, as described in the Book of Acts. Other groups with innovative practices marked English society during the sixteenth and seventeenth centuries. The Familists believed that the knowledge of God was given by direct revelation without the necessity of belief in the infallibility of the Bible and use of the sacraments of Baptism and the Holy Supper. They only allowed remarriage in the advent of widowhood and were highly discreet about their internal practices. The Adamites believed they had recovered the original purity, lost in the fall of man from the Garden of Eden. That's why they were naked. The Mugggletonians and the Grindletonians had a low appreciation for the ability of reason to produce truth and emphasized the usefulness of prophesying through divine revelations. The Philadelphia Society had similar attitudes.

John Bordage (1607-1681), inspired by the mystical ideas of the German Jacob Böhme (1575-1624), believed that he could obtain direct revelations from God about everything that exists. His successor, Jane Leade (1624-1704) claimed to have had a vision of

Paulo: Companhia das Letras, 1987, pp. 30-31.

[130] Ibid., pp. 124-129.

[131] "Thus, the unofficial thinking and action of the Levellers went much further than the constitutional leaders intended to question property in a way, in view of the latter, embarrassing [...] on natural rights is that Gerrard Winstaley would build their communist theories." Ibid., pp. 128-129.

the Virgin Sophia and believed that the Holy Spirit was in the soul. Fifth Kingdom monarchs, on the other hand, when England lost its king in the civil war, believed that the prophecy of the Book of God would be fulfilled in England, with the restoration of the English throne.[132] Another dissident group, but with characteristics different from the ones mentioned above, were the Ranters. Members of this group were typically antinomians.[133] For them, there was no need to fear the Bible and the law of God. To do as he wished was more pious, as they understood it, than to believe in the resurrection of the dead at the end of the world. Being in a brothel, drinking wine, and adulterating was more sacrosanct than taking the Lord's Supper. Shock and blasphemy were the instruments they used to protest against church beliefs and attitudes that they considered oppressive. They should live their lives, free from all fear and all dogma. During the sixteenth century, England was inundated with radicals.

Heterodox Christianity was strongly opposed to established orthodoxy. Ranters, however, promoted more than just a non-conservative Christian life. They sought to demonstrate that there is no difference, just as they understood the relationship between the sacred and the profane, and the Christian and the pagan.[134] Everything was sacred because it was profane, and vice versa. The least radical of the groups hitherto quoted was the Quaker. They

---

[132] Ibid., pp. 36-37.

[133] "In a Ranter meeting of which we have an account (it is true that hostile), the very heterogeneous assistants in their composition met in a tavern, chanted obscene songs about melodies of well-known psalms and ate a lot in common [...] The only name the Ranters seemed to accept for their community was "my flesh one." This term and the fulfillment *"fellow creature"* with which they were addressed were intended to emphasize the union with humanity and even with the whole creation." Ibid., pp. 201, 206.

[134] "Unity with creation, tobacco as "a good creature" of God, thus parodying holy communion: we must never fail to look for the present symbolism in what at first sight seems only to be another extravagant gesture of the radicals of the seventeenth century [...] A compulsive desire to curse and blaspheme [had] overpowered [a ranter] in his youth, but he was able to resist it for good twenty-seven years. Then, however, he tried to make up for lost time. I wanted to say, once, 'to hear a mighty angel (within the man) utter a delicious blasphemy, from those who come with their mouth full,' to hear the preaching of an orthodox minister." Ibid., pp. 202-203.

rejected any leadership in the church. It was to be led by the Holy Spirit alone.

They believed in the revelatory power of the Holy Spirit to lead their lives in spontaneous church meetings. In addition, they rejected political activity and were pacifists.[135] Its major leader, George Fox (1624-1691), was known for his cordial and ascetic personality. The largest group, among the radicals who opposed the Church of England, were known as "Puritans." They were members of various churches, such as Presbyterian, Congregational, and Baptist. They were engaged in the quest to establish a church faithful to the Bible in England, judging the view of the established church as one that had added human imaginations to the Holy Scriptures. They opposed all other groups mentioned above, as well as being opponents of the Socinians, who denied the doctrine of the trinity, and the Shakers, who, in addition to other positions, advocated the need for gender equality. The Puritans wanted, in effect, to create an impact in the country by restoring the forgotten truths, true Christianity. How would this occur?

The Anglicans, members of the established church, did not have a theological position. Puritans were responsible for the real reform in the country. The Puritans also adhered to the Calvinist faith, which they knew was more radical than the Lutheran.

Puritanism, the more extreme side of British Calvinism, had representatives in the political milieu (some members of the House of Lords and the House of Commons were Puritan parliamentarians) and the academic milieu[136] opposing medieval obscurantism.[137]

---

[135] "They do not deny the existence of God or the historical reality of Christ, nor do they deny the existence of heaven and hell. They do not believe that everyone is capable of perfection on this earth. They are not contrary to the authority of magistrates or parents [...] The first official statement in favor of absolute pacifism under any circumstances was pronounced by the Quakers." pp. 233, 237.

[136] "In England, in the sixteenth and seventeenth centuries, the relationship between science and puritanism was narrow [...] Puritanism found many adherents among the newly emancipated class of merchants, artisans, and sailors, then on the rise and which showed much interest in science and technology." HOOYKAAS, R. *The Religion and the Development of Modern Science*, Ibid., pp. 175, 180.

[137] "The Puritans [...] either did not want bishops at all, or they accepted bishops

Strongly Anti-Catholic, the Puritans opposed Aristotelianism in universities. Pedro Ramo took the place of Aristotle in the universities of Cambridge and Oxford. As a professor of logic, Ramo had promoted a new logic, making it more didactic and accessible to the public, since, after the reform, it was not just priests—or people subordinated to the Catholic hierarchy—who had access to academic teaching. Reform in all areas of life, including the educational system, was desired by the Puritans.[138] William Ames (1576-1633), a Puritan theologian, for example, who taught in both England and the Netherlands, was a fervent ramist. Iconoclasts, i.e. idol-destroyers, defenders of private property and the free market, critics of the monarchy and the arts, sought to "glorify God" in all areas of life.

For them, spirituality could not be restricted to the walls of the congregation. The whole of life should be the worship of God, whether it involved a religious celebration, being at work, at school, or in the family. To do so, they had to end what they believed to be Roman Catholic paganism and Christianize the world, breaking with error and bringing truth to the world. More than any other religious group of their day, the Puritans, holding in their minds the idea of the victory of good over evil, of truth over error, of future over the past, knew how to reproduce in practice what they held in theory. They fought for what they believed. They were politically active. The idea of progress inspired them to face the most difficult challenges, even if they were sometimes wrong. Many Puritans favored Bacon's ideas – he had a Puritan mother, Lady Anne Bacon, and, acting as tutors of this family, the figure of preacher John

---

who were overseers, not prelates. They preached a common preaching instead of elaborate liturgy; aspired to reshape the Church in what they believed to be the express teaching of the New Testament, while the other side admitted practices and standards not expressly *forbidden* by Holy Scripture." Ibid., p. 176

[138] "Ramo loved to present his reform as a return to the teachings of classical philosophy [...] Ramo finds it necessary to avoid any mixture of grammar with dialectic and rhetoric. In fact, the first must refer to the problems related to etymologies; the second is the art of creativity and the art of judgment; the third should be limited to the exposition of the techniques of 'style' and 'presentation', as well as the ability to adorn and transmit the material produced by dialectics." ROSSI, Paulo. *The Birth of Modern Science in Europe*, pp. 203-204.

Walsall.[139] In fact, most Puritans did not view science badly. If it did not contradict the Scriptures, and if it existed to demonstrate through observation of nature the marks of the Creator, they saw it as a means of glorifying God. The problem to be addressed was blasphemy: any idea that denied the eternal truths of God revealed in the Bible. The Puritans, in this case, were allied with all other Orthodox Christians. Moreover, the discovery of the New World[140] aroused in European men, including the British, the idea that God had appointed Christians to advance knowledge in the world and to bring Christianity to hitherto unknown peoples.

This was Bacon's religious context. As a prominent English philosopher, he could not avoid the religious problems of his time. Moreover, during the sixteenth and seventeenth centuries religion occupied a prominent place in society. It was not possible to analyze society without an analysis of the predominant religion being carried out. Anglicans, Ranters, Grindletonians, Adamists, Familistas, Muggetonians, Levellers, Quakers, Shakers, Socinians, and Puritans, among others, served as the basis for a new theology in England. Knowing how people would understand faith and God would provide the foundation for the reception of modern science.

---

[139] "Gresham College [...] a meeting place with intellectuals, was regarded as a boiling point of Puritanism, and it is understandable that the writings of Francis Bacon, the great champion of science and technology, were popular in these circles After reason had submitted to the Divine Truth [for the Puritans], learned piety and erudite piety would lead to a 'sublime knowledge.'" HOOYKAAS, R. *The Religion and the Development of Modern Science*, pp. 180-181. For more information on the idea of progress among Puritans, see ibid., p. 181. For more information on the religiosity of Bacon's family see MILLER, Kevin. *The Commonplace Book: The Key to Sir Francis Bacon's Philosophy and Method*, pp. 2-5-6.

[140] "The number of ships with more than 100,000 tons increased from 35 in 1545 to 183 in 1558 and 350 in 1620. The port of London, where ships from Asia and the New World were to be found, from which the expeditions against the traffic of Spanish galleons began, acquired an importance previously unknown. In 1557, the same year that the young Bacon (aged 16) rebels against the Aristotelian culture, Francis Drake repeated Magellan's enterprise and returned to his homeland full of Spanish prey. In 1584 Walter Raleigh founded the first English colony in America, and in the same year the Turkish Company was born in London, from which the Company of the Indies would be born." ROSSI, Paolo. *Francis Bacon: From Magic to Science*, p. 70.

Bacon lived in a time when Anglicans, most of whom had Puritans as their main rivals, and remnants of an Aristotelian heritage were present among Catholics within the Anglican Church. As a Protestant, Bacon was able to combine the idea of God with the idea of progress.

3.2 Bacon and Puritanism: Similarities and Differences

Certainly, "atheist" is not an adjective that can be used to describe Bacon. Despite being heterodox in theology, Bacon considered religion useful to the fellowship of men and the speculative search for the divine. What must be understood, in order to discover the real dimension of the relationship between Bacon and religion, is that science and the scientific method for him were limited. Bacon thought that religion possessed an "area" of human thought that would be inviolable by science.[141]

Did Bacon relativize theology? If so, has it not emptied religion of its content? For the English philosopher, the relation between theology and the legacy of the experimental philosophy of Greece and Rome should be rejected. For example, if the cosmological background of the patristic and scholastic period was based on the Ptolemaic system, Aristotelian physics, Galen's medicine, or other postulates of antiquity, in order to provide a reasonable interpretation of the Scriptures, the very essence of religion would be different. If, therefore, it needed scientists to deal with faith, then there would be no true faith on the one hand, nor true science on the other.

In this sense, it can be argued that Bacon was influenced by the debate in the Late Middle Ages between realists and nominalists. In order not to deviate from the focus of the present investigation, it can be said, succinctly, that the realists defended the substantiality of the universals and the nominalists defended the reduction of substantiality to the individuals, arguing that the universals were no

---

[141] Bacon says in *Valerius Terminus*: "There is in the divine nature both religion and philosophy." BACON, Francis. *The Philosophical Works of Francis Bacon*. New York: Routledge, 2011.

more than names. Exceptions and a middle ground between them were sometimes sought, as in the case of the conceptualists. Ockham's Razor, proposed by the nominalist thinker Guilherme de Ockham (1285-1347), argued that it was necessary to have a philosophy that would eliminate the excess of complexity that did not lead to an obvious truth, or rather that it was necessary to give the simplicity of propositions, because they are better able to deal with particular realities, and the primacy over propositional plurality, which deals with non-existent universal entities. This proposal influenced the Renaissance critique of Scholasticism and Aristotelian logic, which was considered very complex and unproductive.[142] Such nominalism, attacking the postulates of classical logic, also greatly affected theology. Besides Ockham, thinkers such as Gabriel Biel (1425-1495) proposed a theology that did not use reason, as understood by Greek philosophy and classical thinkers, to formulate dogmas.[143] For these nominalist theologians, faith and reason did not conjoin; they remained separate. Nominalism, or at least its reformist spirit, had some influence on the Protestant Reformation. Luther (1483-1546) made praises—although limited—to Ockham. Ramist logic, which sought to replace Aristotelian logic with a simpler logic in Bacon's

---

[142] "In the *Advancement of Learning* of 1605 Bacon says that pride led the scholastics to despise the oracles of the divine word and to dissolve it in the mixture of their inventions; the same arrogant pride which characterizes the theology of the scholastics manifested itself in its philosophy: in the attitude towards nature, in abandoning the works of God, in worshiping the false and deformed images of the world, produced by the mind or extracted from the texts of a few authors. The impiety of scholasticism manifests itself in two directions: in the construction of a rational theology that aims to define and to know the divine essence; in abandoning the great book of nature and works in which God manifested his power." ROSSI, Paolo. *The Science and Philosophy of the Modern*. Trad. br. Álvaro Lorencini. São Paulo: UNESP, 1992. pp. 67-68.

[143] "Medieval thought (also as the 'ideal type') insisted on a universal hierarchy that led to God, and on the acceptance of a transcendence necessary for the understanding of the things of the world. The search for an absolute truth made reason only a 'reflected light', without autonomy [...] In contrast, with the Renaissance, the movement for the hegemony of quantity over quality begins, and the search for immanent laws begins, mathematically formulable. This process was, however, ambiguous, because science and mysticism walked together." WOORTMANN, Klaas. *Religion and Science in the Renaissance*. Brasília: UNB, 1997, pp. 131-132.

England, came from a Protestant:[144] Pedro Ramo.[145] Bacon, in this context, stood not only against Roman Catholicism but also against the influence of philosophy on theology, which had happened in scholastic theology, and even in patristic theology. His argument was that if he did not speak against theology itself, in the wake of reformism and the nominalism of his time, then he proposed a kind of return from theology to its essence.[146] A hermeneutic of reformism and not that of 'beginning from scratch' was what Bacon sought for theology. He did not propose what the later French Revolution did with religion, replacing the Christian calendar with a new calendar and the traditional religion with one that worshiped the goddess Reason, nor did he propose what would later be composed by Auguste Comte (1798-1857) and by positivism. In fact, Bacon sought to reconcile his view of theology with the greater openness to historical review existing in the latitudinal wing of the Anglican Church. In this church there are at least three theological wings: The Catholic wing, the Calvinist wing, and the latitudinal wing. The third wing, which was most suitable for Bacon, was less

---

[144] "What must be emphasized in Ramo's position is, above all, the attempt to insert the issues pertaining to memory in a broader discourse, encompassing not only the elaboration of a useful technique for speakers, lawyers and poets, but also questions concerning method and logic." ROSSI, Paolo. *The Universal Key: Arts of Memorization and Combinatorial Logic from Lulio to Leibniz*. Trad. br. Antonio Angonese. Bauru: EDUSC, 2004, pp. 208-209.

[145] "Ramo loved to present his reform as a return to the teachings of classical philosophy [...] Ramo finds it necessary to avoid any mixture of grammar with dialectic and rhetoric. In fact, the first must refer to the problems related to etymologies; the second is the art of creativity and the art of judgment; the third should be limited to the exposition of the techniques of 'style' and 'presentation', as well as the ability to adorn and transmit the material produced by dialectics." ROSSI, Paolo. *The Birth of Modern Science in Europe*. Trad. br. Antonio Angonese. Bauru: EDUSC, 2001, pp. 203-204.

[146] "Natural philosophy, after the word of God, is the best medicine against superstition, and the most substantial food of faith. Hence, natural philosophy is rightly regarded as the most faithful servant of religion, since one (the Scriptures) makes manifest the will of God, another (natural philosophy) its power [...] It is not of itself to admire that the development of natural philosophy has been curtailed, since religion, which has so much power over men, thanks to the imperfection and jealousy of some, has been drawn against it and predisposed." BACON, Francis. *Novum Organum*, p. 59.

orthodox in theology and more open to the progressive spirit of late medieval intellectuals. In spite of this, Bacon was not a public adversary of what is conventionally called traditional Christianity. It is known that Bacon was not a rebel isolated in the religious context of England.[147]

Although there may be interpretations of Bacon's words that see him as an anti-religious scientist, the English philosopher, read and studied in more detail, reveals himself as not antagonistic to the nominalist school and the context of theological reform in his time. The scientific method was not, for Bacon, the condition of being able to do everything. Aleister Crowley's The Law of Thelema (1875-1947),[148] which reads, "Do what thou wilt, shall be the whole of the law" could not have guided the psychology of methodic formation, nor even the anarchic character of political dissidents of his time, like Ranters. Overcoming paradigms, overcoming boundaries, reaching the once unreachable, among other things, were the yearnings of Bacon. At the same time, however, there was a consciousness of pre-methodological reality, namely the reality of faith.[149]

---

[147] "In their simplicity some [theologians] fear that the deeper investigation of nature will go beyond the limits allowed by their sobriety, transposing, and thereby distorting, the meaning of what the Holy Scriptures say about those who want to penetrate the divine mysteries, for those who turn to the secrets of nature, whose exploitation is by no means interdicted [...] [Theologians] fear that, by example, the movements and changes in philosophy will eventually fall back on religion. Others, at last, seem to fear that the investigation of nature will ultimately subvert or undermine the authority of religion, especially for the ignorant. But these last two fears seem to us to know entirely an animal instinct, as if men, in the recess of their minds and in the secret of their reflections, distrusted and doubted the firmness of religion and the empire of faith over reason and, so they feared the risk of investigating the truth of nature." Ibid., pp. 58-59.

[148] He was an obscure figure who died in the twentieth century, but used the knowledge of Hermeticism and magic existing in Bacon's time for peculiar purposes.

[149] "Bacon, though not a Puritan, had been brought up in the spirit of Elizabethan puritanism [...] The whole scheme of Christian Theology-Creation, Fall, Mediation, and Redemption – was at the base of his philosophical works; there was hardly any sort of argument in which she did not infiltrate. This philosophy fit perfectly with the ideals of the Puritans, especially of the more radical, who wished to Christianize, though not to clericalize, all walks of life [...] Bacon's almost biblical language must have pleased his English contemporaries in

The Puritan movement is considered to be the most anti-Catholic fraction in Calvinism. The struggle against what they believed to be idolatry and the need to carry out reform in England were its most important goals. For them, the Anglican Church had not adhered to the Protestant Reformation as it should. Thus, they thought it was necessary to expand the reformist work within the Anglican Church, which had only undergone a partial reform. It is known that Bacon was not a Puritan. Nevertheless, the apparent radicalism of Baconian reformist thought caught the attention of the Puritans.[150] Puritan representatives in the English parliament looked favorably upon Bacon's proposals, as Bacon recognized in the puritanical spirit—whose motto was *Post Tenebras Lux*—an ally in the quest to overcome England's scholastic past. Puritan Baconianism even made it to New England. The eminent Puritan Cotton Mather (1663-1728) was considered a Baconian. What are the reasons for this relationship between Bacon and Puritanism? There are a few:

1. The two are strongly antagonistic to the immediate past of the European intelligentsia, ruled by Roman Catholicism;
2. The two want a change—in the world that is contemporary to them—greater than the more moderate groups among the reformists;
3. Bacon, by giving theology a status of "discipline of faith," appeals to more radical reformist sectors that reject the "excess of rationalism" in Roman Catholicism;
4. The literalist appeal to biblical interpretation in Puritanism, together with its rejection of Catholic symbolism and

---

general, and to his Puritan compatriots in particular. Many of his characteristic expressions and slogans are found repeatedly in his writings: 'progress of knowledge', 'discovery of a new world', 'new reforms', 'light'. HOOYKAAS, R. *The Religion and the Development of Modern Science*, pp. 180-181.

[150] "God never did a miracle to convert an atheist, because the light of nature would have been enough to make him confess the existence of God; but miracles were done to convert the idolaters and superstitious because no natural light ever manifests the will and the true worship of God. To infer from the contemplation of nature, or on the basis of human knowledge, any certainty or conviction concerning matters of faith is not, in my judgment, safe." BACON, Francis. *The Advancement of Learning* [1605], p. 140.

ritualism, gives its *modus vivendi* a more textual, grammatical, and literary character, to gain political strength allied with the humanist desire to "return to the sources", with technological development achieved by the appearance of the press, and with the help of the nationalist spirit. Bacon, thus, would be more political reformist allied with the Puritan reform.

5. Both are enthusiasts of the reformist spirit that pervaded their world.

As was said in the previous section, however, Bacon is better classified as a member of the latitudinal wing of the Anglican Church. This would be less radical in the judgment of the heterodox aspects of Baconian theology, in addition to being more open to the humanist and Renaissance influences of the late Middle Ages. However, the complexity of Bacon's personality prevents him from restricting himself to a specific group. This is what happens with Puritanism. Such a relationship becomes more evident when one understands the language that Bacon uses to criticize the errors of the ancient thinkers. As a politician and chancellor of King James I, Bacon knew how to make his rhetoric more attractive and popular:

> Sacred Theology (which in our language we call Divine Knowledge) is founded only on the word and the oracle of God, and not in the light of nature: for it is written: *Coeli enarrant gloriam Dei*, but not it is written: *Coeli enarrant voluntatem Dei* [the heavens declare the will of God], but it says: *Ad legem et testimonium: si non fecerint secundam verbum istud* etc. [By teaching and testimony: If they do not speak according to this word etc]. This applies not only to those who concern the moral law correctly interpreted: Love your enemies, do good to those who persecute you, be like your heavenly Father, who pours his rain on the just and the unjust.[151]

The theory of idols is clear evidence of this. The word "idolatry" in Bacon's time was extremely common among the Puritans.[152] For

---

[151] BACON, Francis. *The Advancement of Learning* [1605], p. 310.
[152] "Puritanism and New Philosophy therefore have much in common: anti-

them, it was necessary to rid the Christian world of the idolatry they believed existed in Roman Catholicism, and thus to make it appear that the influence of Roman paganism on Christianity was destroyed and the Jewish legacy of that restored faith. Bacon turned out to be iconoclastic, but not a literal iconoclast.

His iconoclasm was symbolic and rhetorical. Symbolic because, when he used the term idol, he did not refer to an entity worshiped in religious temples, and therefore not an idol in the conventional and literal sense.[153] Rhetorical because, in describing himself as opposed to idols,[154] he made his discourse more contemporary, attractive, and popular among the politically dissident minds of his day. The idols of the tribe, the cave, and the theater, rather being than an attempt by Bacon to undertake a critique of epistemology, logic, and antiquity, are symbols of a rhetorical device conducive to the reformist era Bacon belonged to. The similarities between Bacon's political project and the Puritans can also be noted when one studies the reasons why the English philosopher undertakes his vision of social progress. Both the Puritans and Bacon possessed an optimistic eschatology.[155] In fact, as will be seen in the next section,

---

authoritarianism, optimism about human possibilities, rational empiricism, the emphasis on experience [...] This does not necessarily imply that Puritanism as such would produce many highly qualified scientists. Here the point under discussion belongs to the sociology of religion: has Puritanism, in fact, created a spiritual climate conducive to the cultivation and freedom of science? The affirmative answer to this question is not an invention of modern sociologists." HOOYKAAS, R. *The Religion and Development of Modern Science*, p. 185.

[153] "There is no solidity in logical or physical notions. Substance, quality, action, passion, not even being, are safe notions. Much less are those of heavy, light, dense, rare, moist, dry, generation, corruption, attraction, repulsion, element, matter, form, and the like. All are fantastic and ill-defined [...] The idols that block the human mind are of four kinds. In order to present them better, we have signed names to them, namely: Idols of the Tribe, Cave Idols, Idols of the Forum, and Idols of the Theater [...] the formation of notions and axioms by the true induction is undoubtedly the appropriate remedy to ward off and repel the idols." BACON, Francis. *Novum Organum* [1620], pp. 15, 21.

[154] For McLuhan, the four idols of Francis Bacon already appear, so to speak, in Roger Bacon. See McLuhan, Eric. *Francis Bacon's Theory of Communication and Media*. McLuhan Studies, Issue 4, Toronto, 1999.

[155] "For the Puritans of the seventeenth century, the Kingdom of Man

Bacon brings theological concepts to his scientific project. Hence it can be said that there is an influence of Puritan eschatological optimism (in general) on Bacon's optimism regarding the scope of his scientific method. For him, the king should sponsor progress, especially through the Royal Society. If Bacon diverged from the Puritan theological orthodoxy that defined (in its own sense of the word) progress, at least the spirit of the "new" was somewhat present in both. From the point of view of Roman Catholicism and the proponents of a restoration of the medieval world, both groups worked towards the same goal.

Later, after Bacon's death, the Puritan Revolution under Oliver Cromwell (1599-1658) began. If the Congregationalists were generally opposed to the monarchy, the Scottish Puritan Presbyterians were the ones who helped to restore it under Charles II. This spirit, although divergent in theology, resembles that of Bacon politically.

3.3 Epistemology, Divine Philosophy, and Method

In *The Advancement of Learning* Bacon divides philosophy into Divine Philosophy, Natural Philosophy, and Human Philosophy. According to Divine Philosophy, atheism is refuted because of the knowledge of the rudiments of divinity in nature. Bacon says the following on the Divine Philosophy of Natural Theology:

> With regard to Divine Philosophy or Natural Theology, we will say that it is this knowledge or rudiment of knowledge about God that can be obtained from the contemplation of its creatures, knowledge that, in truth, can be called divine in relation to the object and natural in relation to light. The limits

---

complemented the Kingdom of God; after reason had submitted to the Divine Truth, erudite piety and pious erudition would lead to a 'sublime knowledge'. It was a time of great expectations. The discovery of a new geographical world in the previous century would lead, according to Francis Bacon, to the discovery of a new intellectual world. John Wilkins [the Anglican theologian], in which he stated 'that there may be another inhabitable world on the Moon' and that there is 'possibility of a journey there' (1638), had anticipated the discovery of a new world in the sky." HOOYKAAS, R. *The Religion and the Development of Modern Science*, pp. 181-182.

of this knowledge are sufficient to refute atheism, but not to inform religion.[156]

In order to understand the context of this Divine Philosophy or Natural Theology in Bacon's thought, it will be necessary to delve into the details of the other two philosophies. This detour is necessary because it is associated with the theme and is necessary for understanding his philosophy. Bacon divides Natural Philosophy into two parts, namely the Inquisition of Causes and the Production of Effects. He also deals with the Law of Cause and Effect, which, however, cannot be applied before the empirical process. It still deals with the Speculative and Operative modes of knowledge, which are interconnected, but the experimental relationship between man and nature is the condition of speculation. If, for Bacon, the natural philosopher has "ascending experiments to the invention of causes, and descending from causes to the invention of new experiments, there is a need to separate these two moments, namely, what goes from experiments to causes and causes to new experiments, to better develop this philosophy."[157] Bacon also subdivides Natural Philosophy into Physics and Metaphysics, and the first must study the Material and Efficient Cause and the second, the Formal and Final Cause.[158] Both, however, contribute to the perfection of Natural Philosophy. Physics is also divided into three parts, the first referring to the Configuration of Things, the second to the Principles and Origins of Things, and the third to the Varieties and Particularities of Things. The first two are related, therefore, to the unity of matter and the last to the diffusion of matter. The function of Metaphysics was to investigate the Formal and Final Causes.[159] He, however,

---

[156] BACON, Francis. *The Advancement of Learning* [1605], p. 160.

[157] "Physics has three parts, two of which refer to joined or collected nature, and the third study of diffuse or distributed nature. Nature can be gathered, either in a single whole, or in principles or seeds. So the first doctrine is that relating to the Contexture or Configuration of Things [...] The second is the doctrine of the Principles and Origins of things. The third is the doctrine concerning all Variety and Particularity of things, whether it be their different substances, or their different qualities and natures." See, Ibid., p. 147.

[158] Ibid., p. 146.

[159] See Ibid., pp. 146-147.

regards the investigation of the Forms as "the most deserving of being sought, if it were possible to be found."[160] Metaphysical work is, therefore, according to him, part of the Philosophy of Nature. Bacon claims that the process of investigating the formal causes of each substance is difficult. The way each substance presents itself is varied, so its analysis is complex. For example, he says that "it would not be possible nor useful to seek in general the forms of the sounds or voices that make up words, which by composition and transposition of letters are infinite." In addition, he says, in relation to the study of the final causes, that because they are "mixed with other physical investigations" also were not correctly[161] studied[162] throughout the

---

[160] See Ibid., pp. 146-147.

[161] "The Forms of Substance, I mean, as they now appear multiplied by combination and transplantation, are so complicated that it is not possible to inquire into them, just as it would neither be possible nor useful to seek in general the forms of the sounds or voices that make up the words, which by composition and transposition of letters are infinite. But on the other hand, one can easily inquire into the forms of those sounds or voices which make the simple letters, which, once known, manifest and lead to the forms of all words, which consist and are composed of them [...] part of Metaphysics I do not find it worked out and done, which does not surprise me, because I do not think it through the investigation process that has been used, because (and this is the root of every mistake) we have abandoned very prematurely and moved away from the particulars [...] The treatment of the final causes mixed with the others in the physical investigations numbed the severe and diligent inquiry into all real and physical causes, and gave men occasion to dwell on these merely pleasing and specious causes, with great brake and prejudice to other discoveries." Ibid., pp. 148-149, 152.

[162] Prima Philosophy or Supreme Philosophy and Metaphysics, which until now have been confused as one thing, are two distinct things. For it was put as the progenitor or common ancestor of all knowledge, and I have now introduced it as a branch or descendant of Natural Science [....] The question now arises of what remains for Metaphysics, on which I can safely to preserve the idea of antiquity up to this point, that physics must study what is inserted in matter and therefore is transitory, and metaphysics, that which is abstract and fixed. And also that physics must deal with what only an existence and a movement presupposes in nature, and metaphysics must deal with what supposes, moreover, in nature a reason, an understanding, and a plan [...] Just as Philosophy Natural in general we divided it into Inquisition of Causes and subdivided it into Inquisition of Causes and Production of Effects, so that part that refers to the Inquisition of the causes we subdivided according to the established and correct division of the causes:

ages. Mathematics, especially Pure Mathematics, is seen by Bacon as essential for the understanding of Metaphysics. Bacon goes on to say that "Pure Mathematics belongs to those sciences which deal with the determinate Quantity, separated from every axiom of natural philosophy."[163] To end the analysis of the philosophy of nature, Bacon says one must investigate oneself. Self-knowledge is, for Bacon, the "final and determinate, separated from every axiom of the term of natural philosophy," where the knowledge of nature ends and knowledge about man begins. Epistemology here joins praxis, in the social and political world. Bacon, entering into Human Philosophy, shows that this begins where the Philosophy of Nature ends; therefore, the knowledge of nature consequently leads to the true knowledge of humanity. Just as the end of Natural Philosophy is Human Philosophy, the end of Human Philosophy is Civil Knowledge.[164]

With the end of this digression, one arrives at the following conclusions: How can Metaphysics and Mathematics be useful to knowledge if the true knowledge is only possible with the inductive method? How can Natural Theology be useful if it does not bring real knowledge, such as the knowledge acquired by the method? How can Human Philosophy and Natural Philosophy, without method, be treated as a source of knowledge? These incongruities permeate the whole of Baconian thought and render problematic the idea that he was only a "philosopher of method" or a "philosopher of induction." Before even dealing with Philosophy in *The Advancement of Learning*, Bacon had already divided the History of Nature into three, namely the History of the Creatures, History of the Wonders, and History of the Arts. Civil History had been

---

one of the parts, that is the Physics, studies and deals with Material and Efficient Causes, and the other, which is Metaphysics, deals with Formal and Final Causes [...] Physics [...] is situated in a term or distance between Natural History and Metaphysics. For Natural History describes the varieties of things, Physics, the fixed and constant causes." Ibid., pp. 145-146.

[163] See Ibidem, p. 155.

[164] "The prudence of the legislator is not only about the standard of justice, but also about its application [...] I have concluded part of the knowledge about Civil Knowledge, and with civil knowledge I have concluded the Human Philosophy, and with the Human Philosophy, General Philosophy." pp. 306-307.

divided into Memorials, Complete Histories, and Antiquities. The Just and Perfect History had been defined as Chronicles, Lives, and Narratives or Stories, as well as dealing with the History of Times, History of Cosmography, and True History. Added to this was the division of Poetry into Narrative, Representative, and Allusive. All this reveals a paradox in Baconian thought. If his criticism of the idols of thought and his criticism of the ancients were taken into account, there would be only one truly certain thought in Bacon when he proceeded to the inductive method. For, if knowledge is reduced to the application of the method, man is epistemologically prevented from making correct statements about anything, for only what is experienced by the method can be considered factual. Thus, Bacon could not discuss mathematics, metaphysics, theology, philosophy, physics, and undertake these innumerable subdivisions of these themes discussed above, since they were not tested by method. In light of this, there are three possibilities:

1. Bacon is a philosopher unable to know the contradictions of his thought and therefore irrelevant;
2. One should ignore the contradictions of his thought and reduce the relevance of his thought to the elaboration of his inductive method;
3. One must study the philosopher in his completeness, recognizing his limitations, and seek to discover the idea behind the dichotomy method-speculation.

The third option is advocated here. One can easily see speculation and method united in Bacon's works. As we have seen, *The Advancement of Learning* is proof of this. In it the philosopher asserts that the study of forms by metaphysics—which is somewhat aided by mathematics and has a purpose other than physics, which studies the configuration of things—is speculative, and as such its conclusions are only theoretical, in the sense of being in the field of probability and never of objectivity. The same can be said, roughly, of Natural Theology or Divine Philosophy, of Human Philosophy, of History, with its subdivisions, and also in regard to Poetry. Even Physics, which like Metaphysics is part of Natural Philosophy, and which it highlights as an experimental discipline, should possess dogmas only after the inductive method is implanted – Bacon thus draws from it the idea that it has an inherent exactitude, since in practice the extension of the use of the method will include speculation.

In the face of all this, it is evident that,

1. There is in Bacon, in spite of the criticism of idols, a kind of knowledge outside that of method. It is not questioned here that this possibility will be unconscious;

2. The knowledge coming from method is safe and objective. Knowledge outside the method is speculative, not secure. Before exploring this fact, one must develop Bacon's ideas in his critique of idols.[165]

The idols are four, those of the tribe, the cave, the forum, and the theater. The first are the prejudices inherent in the human species itself, proper to the senses, when not regulated by method; the second[166] are those in which the individuals, interacting with the

---

[165] "The idols of the tribe are founded on human nature itself, on the tribe itself or human species. The assertion that the senses of man are the measure of things is false. Quite the contrary, all perceptions, both of the senses and of the mind, are analogous to human nature and not to the universe. The human intellect is like a mirror that unequivocally reflects the rays of things and thereby distorts and corrupts them." BACON, Francis. *Novum Organum* [1620], p. 21.

[166] "The idols of the cave are those of men as individuals. For, each one—besides the aberrations proper to human nature in general—has a cave or cave that intercepts and corrupts the light of nature: either because of the unique nature of each individual; whether due to education or conversation with the other; either by reading the books or by the authority of those who respect and admire; either by difference of impressions, according to whether they occur in a preoccupied and predisposed mood or in an equanimous and tranquil mood; in such a way that the human spirit—as it is disposed in each one—is something various, subject to multiple disturbances, and to some extent subject to chance. Therefore, Heraclitus proclaimed well that men seek in their little worlds and not in the great or universal [...] The idols of the cave have their origin in the peculiar constitution of the soul and body of each; and also in education, in habit, or in fortuitous events [...] Men cling to the sciences and to certain matters, or because their authors or discoverers believed, or because they were very committed and familiar with them. But this kind of man, when he engages in philosophy and general speculation, distorts and corrupts them in favor of his former fantasies. This can be especially noted in Aristotle who so submits his natural philosophy to

environment and reacting to education, become incapable of knowing the reality of things; the third[167] are those acquired by language, which, on the other hand, help man in the search for knowledge, becomes confused with his own things, that is, from the middle to the end, and he becomes an end in itself and an "idol"; the last one[168] is derived from fallacious (and fanciful) theories about

---

logic that made it almost useless and more shaken to contention." Ibid., pp. 21-22, 27.

[167] "The idols of the forum are of all the most disturbing: they insinuate themselves in the intellect thanks to the covenant of words and names. Men, in fact, believe that their reason governs words. But it also happens that words come back and reflect their forces on the intellect, which makes philosophy and science sophistical and inactive. Words, almost always taking on the meaning which the vulgar inculcates them, follow the line of division of things which are most powerful to the vulgar intellect. However, when the keenest intellect and the most diligent observation wish to transfer these lines so that they coincide more adequately with their nature, the words oppose [...] Hence [the idols of the forum] that the great and solemn disputes between learned men often end up in controversies around words and names, in which case it would be better (according to the use and wisdom of mathematicians) to restore order, beginning with definitions. And even the definitions cannot totally remedy this evil, when it comes to natural and material things, since the definitions themselves consist of words and words generate words. Where it is necessary to resort to private facts and to their own orders and series." Ibid., pp. 28-29.

[168] "There are idols that have immigrated to the minds of men through the various philosophical doctrines and also by the vicious rules of demonstration. They are the idols of the theater: it seems that the philosophies adopted or invented are other fables, produced and represented, which include fictional and theatrical worlds [...] We do not think only of philosophical systems, of their universality, but also number. For if, for so many centuries, the human mind had not been occupied with religion and theology; and if civil governments (especially monarchies) had not been so adverse to novelty, even in philosophical speculations – to such an extent that the men who attempt them are subject to risks, to the loss of their fortune, and without any prize, expose themselves to contempt and hatred; if this were not so, no doubt many other philosophical sects and other theories would not have been introduced, such as flourished so greatly among the Greeks. For, just as many theories of heaven can be formulated from that of heavenly phenomena; even more so, on the phenomena of which philosophy is concerned, many dogmas can be founded and constituted. And the fables of this theater are the same as in the theater of the poets. The narratives made for the scene are more orderly and elegant and delight more than the true narratives taken from history." Ibid., pp. 22-23, 30-31.

reality – as well as grounded in the mere obedience to the authority of the one who teaches them. If, however, man got rid of all these idols, which are the causes of all evils, what will he have left? Perfection. If the individual does not possess a fallacious theory, or a vice of language, or is negatively influenced by the environment, or possess any vice inherent to humanity, he will become "nonhuman", that is, the limitation or finitude that opens to the possibility of error and which characterizes humanity will be absent, so that the term "human"—understood in the common sense of the term—cannot, by logic, be applied to it. This implication, also not perceived by Bacon, prevents him from carrying out the intention of making the common man neutral to the inductive method. If this were possible, as Bacon wanted, this man would be a *tabula rasa*—even after a lifetime of experiments—to be written by method. If there is no real neutrality, one can speak only of a *virtual* neutrality, in the sense that the naked man of the idols is neutral *in relation to or compared* to the idolatrous man. However, his neutrality, although Bacon did not know it, is not a void in the real sense. The approximate contemporary example is the concept of the vacuum in physics. Such a word, while it seems to denote a real emptiness, is not. Then, what is the *thing* that remains in the neutral man, devoid of idols and prepared for method, in Bacon? Answering this question is not easy. Here it is speculated that an appeal to faith or intuition would not be a mistake. This thesis would also solve the problem of Bacon paradoxically refusing to treat religion as a sphere that could be abolished by science.[169] He also supports the influence of mysticism on his thought, since, for the Hermetic tradition, is not seen as an antonym of the absolute, as if it were an absolute nothingness. Thus, this faith or intuition would be nothing more than a kind of nullification or emptying of man in submission to the absolute, method being the way which the absolute was revealed to him.

---

[169] "The application of human reason to religion is of two kinds: the first refers to the conception and apprehension of the mysteries of God that have been revealed to us: the second, to the deduction and derivation of doctrine and guidance from them. The first extends to the mysteries themselves: but how? By way of illustration, not by way of argument. The second consists of proof and argument." BACON, Francis. *The Advancement of Learning*[1605], pp. 311-312.

3.4 The Theologization of Science

As stated in the preceding section, Bacon could not escape the fact that, despite his wish to apply himself to the method, he intuited a reality in which he did not prove *posteriori* and is thus credulous before it. Hence, the argument that there is in Bacon an absent intuition of later abstractionism, of subsequent explanations, or of simple faith—and not understood—in a previous reality, in which the neutral man (he has no idols) prepares for the method. A further thesis follows: this intuitive or fideistic presupposition contributed to the English philosopher gives the method a metaphysical and theological status. The probability that he is not aware of this is great, and therefore it is wiser to argue that he did it unconsciously, since it is contradictory to give the method a metaphysical and theological status before being tested – which he did even when he criticized ancient authors. The fact, however, is that Bacon did this.[170] What then, are the theological and metaphysical components of the method in Bacon? We can list five:

1. Science as a means of Grace or Enlightenment;
2. The overcoming of the Original Sin by Science;
3. The revelation through the Science of the hidden absolute;
4. Science as *gnosis*;
5. Science as liberation from idolatry (eschatology).

---

[170] Unlike Comte, who used the priest figure in the Positivist Catechism, the sages of the House of Solomon (figures who refer to the Temple and the priesthood), as seen in the first chapter, were not for Bacon characters of an era in which religion would be overcome, that is, they were not an archetypal species of positivist priests. Bacon knew that the priests of the ancient world generally sought a more scientific knowledge than that of the common people – among the Hebrews, for example, the healed ones of leprosy were only "freed" from the status of impurity after the priest's evaluation. What the English author wanted, in "thesis", was a confluent separation between religion and science itself. See ROSSI, Paolo. *Shipwrecks without Spectators: The Idea of Progress*, p. 41; COMTE, Augusto. *Positivist Catechism*. Trad. br. José Arthur Giannotti and Miguel Lemos. São Paulo: New Cultural, 1991; See VIEIRA, Raymundo. *Historical Roots of Western Medicine*. São Paulo: Editora Fap-Unifesp, 2012; See CHINCHILLA, Anastasio. *Anales Historicos de la Medicina en General*. Valencia: Press of Lopez Y Compania, 1841.

In regard to the first point, theology is a means for Grace in those who act as mediators for divine salvation on earth. For Bacon, science had the function of saving humanity from mistakes derived from ignorance. It would bring not only knowledge but peace and social harmony. This becomes more evident in the second point: it being known that in theology, original sin made it impossible for humanity to know salvation as good and pleasurable truth. Bacon, giving science a status of grace, believes that it cannot only rid man of errors made by sin but also go beyond theologians, even overcoming original sin and leading humanity to absolute knowledge. In the third point the thesis of the theologization of science in Bacon becomes even clearer: theology utilizes divine revelation, that is, the belief that religious knowledge deals with a category of knowledge that cannot be explained by human reason, although many theologians defend the compatibility between faith and reason. Similarly, the teleology that Bacon gives to method, judging it to be the minister of knowledge and liberator of progress from error, puts him on a plateau where he cannot be questioned. How does this happen? For Bacon, all social ills are also epistemological evils, that is, erroneous methods of knowledge lead to erroneous practice. True knowledge can only be acquired by its inductive method. Bacon says that the end and goal of science were wrongly described by men.[171] But how can he know what the end of science is if his inductive method has not even been put into practice? He then falls into a visible contradiction, as if hidden in kind of shadow, there should be an absolute and certain knowledge of reality as a kind of enlightenment. It is precisely this enlightened knowledge, that knowledge of the absolute, once hidden, that is performative *gnosis*, petition of principle or circular argument. If all erroneous knowledge is due to the non-use of its method, the validity of this method cannot be questioned, since one

---

[171] "The end and goal of science have been misplaced by men. But, though well placed, the route chosen is erroneous and impractical. And it is astounding to anyone who has been warned to consider matter, to the effect that no mortal has been careful or tempted to trace and extend to the human intellect a path from the senses and well-founded experience, on the contrary, whether everything has been abandoned or the darkness of tradition, or the vortex and swirl of arguments, or fluctuations and deviations of chance and a vague and unruly experience." BACON, Francis. *Novum Organum* [1620], p. 149.

would always come (unequivocally) to a misunderstanding of it, from the influence of an erroneous method. The method thus has a teleology, a mission, which is to lead humanity to the liberation of idols and to progress through the discovery of the truth that is hidden in nature, that is, through the absolute knowledge of the reality given by the true induction. As argued in the first chapter, the knowledge-gnosis of what lies behind this phenomena is scientific knowledge, or, as stated in the fourth point, of science as gnosis.[172] This is the knowledge that liberates, illuminates, reveals and initiates man into another realm of reality, which makes him face the world from the knowledge of the absolute. The fifth and last point is that the final result of the application of the method combats an evil, epistemological idolatry, but the method does not present itself as just another combatant of this idolatry, but as its sole combatant, since without it no one can obtain this absolutely efficient result:[173]

> One day, two of our companions were invited to the Family Feast, as they called it. It is a very natural, pious and venerable custom, which shows that the nation is composed of all courtesies, and consists of the following: any man who lives to see thirty descendants of his living together, and all of them older than three years, can make a feast at the expense of the State [...] There is no nation under the skies as chaste as Bensalem, or so free

---

[172] "The reform of knowledge is presented by Bacon as an interpretation of Christianity. *Instauratio* was also set up as an attempt to regain what sin had taken, as a return to a distant and lost past, the old and happy conditions of life. The advance of knowledge is a long and difficult path that seeks to bring the man close to his original state of perfection. The future is also the fulfillment of an ancient promise." ROSSI, Paolo. *Shipwrecks without Spectators: The Idea of Progress*, p. 41.

[173] "The origin of human sin is not the relation between man and knowledge in the realm of the science of good and evil. In other words, human sin originates in the ethical realm, the proud man intended to have a power similar to that of God. Bacon believes that before the Fall man had been endowed by the divine goodness with such a perfection that allowed him to fully know nature, for the human mind had the ability to reflect the universe. Now, with the Fall, both man and nature are from now on imperfect, subject to corruption. Between man and world an abyss was created. Thus the human mind has become an 'enchanted mirror', falsifying, deforming, altering nature." *The Experimental Philosophy in Eighteenth-Century England: Francis Bacon and Robert Boyle*, p. 97.

from corruption and clumsiness. It is the virgin nation of the world [...] Among them, there are no brothels, dissolute houses, no courtesans, or anything of the sort. They are astonished at how you are in Europe [land where the method is not applied; imperfect; fall], you allow such things.[174]

Here there are mystical influences,[175] already discussed in the first section, on Puritan theology and the latitudinal movement of the Anglican Church,[176] but which need to be developed upon now. This wing of Anglicanism is admittedly progressive and had members influenced by humanism, by rebirth, and even more skeptical elements of the late Middle Ages. For example, the latitudinal Anglican theologian John Wilkins (1614-1672) was already demonstrating his progressive view of reality by claiming it is possible for man to live off planet earth. As one who undertook a theological science or non-practical heterodox scientific theology, Bacon found himself in the wake of the progressive ideas of this ward, but at the same time, unlike other members of the ward, he flirted with Puritanism, a morally conservative or even fundamentalist movement. This level of complexity, whether of his personality or his ideas alone, made him embrace a diversity of ideas greater than

---

[174] BACON, Francis. *New Atlantis* [1624], pp. 254, 258-259. The additions in brackets are ours.

[175] "Bacon contrasts with the biblical allegorism a different conception of nature. However, it does not absolutely exclude the presence, in the sacred text, of true and proper axioms of nature and of cosmological and astronomical doctrines. Leviticus seems to contain such axioms [...] In the person of Solomon, Bacon sees not only the composer of remarkable moral parables, but also the natural author of plants and animals. But there remains the fact that Bacon resolutely rejects every 'natural philosophy' which is based on the allegorical reading of the sacred texts. This meant departing from the themes of exemplarism and symbolism, so widespread in the philosophical tradition and still alive in the seventeenth century; contained the refusal of an image of the world understood as explictio of infinite divine complication; carried the denial of all doctrine of the analogism of being and the reaffirmation of absolute divine transcendence." ROSSI, Paolo. *The Science and Philosophy of the Modern.* Trad. br. Álvaro Lorencini. São Paulo: UNESP, 1992, p. 73.

[176] Theologically more flexible movements to less orthodox ideas from the point of view of other Christian traditions.

those commonly accepted by Anglican latitudinarianism, ranging from fundamentalism to progression, from mystique to a seemingly skeptical discourse on religious discourse. More than that, he apparently was not aware that the complexity of his statements put him in an eclectic field, in which the way method relates to assumptions became difficult to decipher:

> The conditions for natural science have become more arduous and dangerous because of the sums and methods of [the] theology of the scholastics. The latter, as he fulfilled them, systematically ordered theology, and gave it the form of an art, and combined, with the body of religion, the contentious and thorny philosophy of Aristotle, rather than the convenient [...] Natural philosophy, later of the word of God, is the best medicine against superstition, and the most substantial food of faith [in this the Protestant religion may be superior to that of the scholastics].[177]

Was Bacon a deist? If deism is understood as the doctrine according to which the universe-forming deity allows it to be guided by its own laws, there being thus no miracle-working or divine interventionism in nature, then, at first sight, it seems, that Bacon was a deist. However, deism is not the best definition for the philosopher's complex position. The deist conception of the divine is better grounded theoretically with the advent of Newtonian and Cartesian mechanics and anti-mysticism. Bacon's thought, on the contrary, despite the apparent mechanism provoked by his rhetoric as to the inductive method, is influenced by mysticism, so that sometimes he confuses the concepts of "divine" and "nature," having a juxtaposition between them.

An example of this is his concept of liberation from the idols by the knowledge of nature. For him, there would be something divine, something essentially good, in nature. This thought cannot be defined as pantheistic. The insistence on the separation of theology from science, even if it were not applied in practice to his thought,

---

[177] BACON, Francis. *Novum Organum* [1620], pp. 58-59.

is a visible sign that he understood that the divine was not reduced to nature, the object of scientific inquiry. If therefore, his thinking is heterodox from the point of view of classical Western theism, it oscillates between it and pantheism, which is the doctrine according to which the divine penetrates the world without being reduced to it, and is different to the teachings of pantheistic doctrine.

3.4.1. THE CREATION OF THE WORLD IN SIX DAYS

North[178] argues there is an intrinsic relationship between the *Instauratio Magna* proposed by Bacon and the *Book of Genesis*, or, more precisely, between the six parts of the establishment and the six days of the creation of the world. Indeed, Bacon's study has led one to believe that it is a fact that the division of the *Instauratio Magna* into six parts did not occur randomly, but rather had a hexameric perspective of the creation reported in *Genesis*. Also, the use of the number six by Bacon is not restricted to *Instauratio*. The *House of Solomon*, orchestrated in *New Atlantis*, is called the *Six Day Work School*. In the ancient world there were seven known planets, and the seventh day was the day of rest for God after the six days of creation, which may indicate that Bacon thought that the end of the great establishment would be the rejoicing of man before the perfect mastery over the cosmos. North also investigates the rhetorical style used by Bacon to address King James I in *The Advancement of Learning* and thinks that Bacon saw his king as a kind of Moses or Hermes, a monarch worthy of undertaking a job fecundity for true knowledge. In fact, by writing to the monarch, Bacon not only compared him to Hermes,[179] but also compared the rest from knowledge to *Shabbat*, which is the seventh-day rest for the Jews, to the planet Saturn – which, for ancient cosmology, was not only related to the heavenly sphere, but also to the divine. In this context the planet is used by Bacon for rest and contemplation, that is, as

---

[178] See NORTH, J. *The Six Day of Creation and Francis Bacon's Great Instauration: Sacred Creativity and the Six Days Work in Bacon*. Francis Bacon Society, Baconiana, Volume 1, No. 3, England, 2009.

[179] BACON, Francis. *The Advancement of Learning* [1605], p. 18.

rest after the work of knowing acting on the real. He contrasts it to Jupiter. While Saturn is the planet of contemplation, Jupiter is the planet of action.[180] In the preface to the *Instauratio Magna*, Bacon elaborates on its hexameric plane. The six parts in which he divided the installation are:

1. The division of the sciences;
2. *Novum Organum* or directives for the interpretation of nature;
3. The phenomenon of the universe or the experimental and natural history for the foundation of Philosophy;
4. The graduation (or ladder) of knowledge;
5. The anticipators or anticipation of Second Philosophy;
6. Second Philosophy or Active Science.[181]

In order to draw an analogy between the six stages of *Instauratio* and his days of creation, North proceeds as follows: compare each day of creation with each proposed stage of Bacon. The first day with the first step, the second day with the second step and so on. First, the six days of creation in ascending order will be set here:

1. Creation of Heaven and Earth. The earth was formless and empty. Light, day and night;
2. Creation of the firmament. Divisions of waters, both above and below;
3. Separation between dry land and seas. Creation of trees and other organic lives;
4. Creation of the sun, moon, and stars;
5. Creation of marine animals and birds;
6. Creation of terrestrial animals, of man and woman.[182]

The creation of Heaven and Earth corresponds to the initial and

---

[180] See Ibidem, p. 62.
[181] NORTH. *The Six Day of Creation and Francis Bacon's Great Instauration: Sacred Creativity and the Six Days Work in Bacon*.
[182] See Ibid.

abstract division of the sciences, but especially to the fact that light and illumination are essential to bring order to chaos since light is superior to darkness, and that the enlightened order organizes the disorder covered by darkness (1). The creation of the firmament corresponds to the interpretation of nature and to the principles of logic (2). The separation between land and sea corresponds to the separation between philosophy and other types of science—one may even speak of the separation of theory and practice—and the beginning of experimentalism and method (3). The creation of the sun, the moon, and the stars corresponds to the idea of the "ladder" or degree of knowledge since the Kabbalah associates celestial figures with perfections and knowledge to a ladder, as well as the ladder of Jacob, which unites Earth to the heavenly world (4). In spite of the logical connections made here, it is in point 5 and in point 6 that North sees as a clear resemblance between the two, since on the fifth day of creation marine animals and birds are created, culminating in the creation of terrestrial animals and man and of women in the sixth, which corresponds to the elevation of the anticipation of Second Philosophy (5) to the full establishment of this Second Philosophy, which is also called Active Science (6), since it is to man, as head of creation, given to *Imago Dei* and science, with the scientist being the true restorer of the original human status – man, so to speak, with a perfection similar to that of angelic beings.[183]

North, dealing with a posthumously published writing by Bacon called *Baconiana*, points out that in this work, there is a fragment called *Abecedarium Novum Naturae*, in which Bacon makes a series of inquiries about science – called *Inquisitions*. The fragmented text provides excerpts ranging from inquisitions 67 to 78. It turns out that it is based on these inquisitions in the twenty-four letters of the Greek alphabet. Taken deductively, the first inquisition would be the alpha, the twenty-fourth the omega, the twenty-fifth the double alpha, and so on, so that the forty-ninth would be the triple-alpha, and the fifty-third would be the fourfold alpha and the beginning of the fourth circular path of the alphabet. In these inquisitions the number six also stands out. There are six metaphysical questions

---

[183] See Ibid., p.1.

raised by Bacon:
- 73rd Inquisition: On Being and Non-Being.
- 74th Inquisition: On the Possible and the Impossible.
- 75th Inquisition: On Much and Little.
- 76th Inquisition: On the Durable and the Transitory.
- 77th Inquisition: On the Natural and the Monstrous.
- 78th Inquisition: On the Natural and the Artificial.[184]

The relationship of these six metaphysical questions to the six days of creation is also obvious to North. The Being and the Not-Being correspond to the first day of creation, in which the Being creates from nothing (1). The Possible and the Impossible correspond to the second day, that of the creation of the firmament, because the gradation of possibilities, which includes impossibility, extends as far as the act of creating extends (2). The Much and the Little correspond to the third day, that of the separation of the waters from the dry land, from the creation of organic life, since it postulates the diversity of things, which are "many" and "few" (3). The Durable and the Transient correspond to the fourth day, that of the creation of the sun, the moon, and the stars since the heavenly bodies are considered bodies which at least have a closer connection with the divine and eternal world than the purely material world and "terrain" (4). The Natural and the Monstrous correspond to the fifth day, that of the creation of marine animals and birds, because certain beings, considered as monstrous, like the Leviathan, were related to the sea, and the air sphere was also a sphere related to demonic entities (5). The Natural and the Artificial correspond to the last day, the day of the creation of the terrestrial animals and the man and the woman, because man is the being who undertakes the artifice of the manufacture, is *homo faber* (6).[185]

What about North's theses on Bacon presented above? Bacon was a connoisseur of gematria—the science of numbers in Judaism— and united Moses and Hermes in their philosophy? Although some

---

[184] See Ibidem, p. 1.
[185] See Ibidem, p.1.

of North's logical deductions may be contested and not all numerical equivalences are accepted by the academic eye, North is correct in drawing a relationship between Bacon and Jewish, Hermetic, Christian mysticism. Since this is the main basis of his thesis, it is necessary to be positive in the evaluation of his arguments, approving them in his conjuncture.

3.5 Bacon, Eschatology, and Roman Catholicism

The fifth point on the theologization of science in Bacon, which deals with the liberation of man from idolatry by science, as stated in the previous section, has an eschatological dimension not yet developed. Certainly, Bacon developed a conception of the method which had, even if he did not admit it, an eschatological dimension. In the first place, he admitted the existence of the Fall. It was this Fall that made it impossible for man to achieve absolute knowledge and led him to epistemological idolatry, which replaced absolute truth by an absolutization of error. The destiny of man without the inductive method was, therefore, to construct idols over idols, that is, epistemological errors about epistemological errors, and thus, as in Bacon, epistemology is associated with political praxis, and bad knowledge would lead to social chaos. The history of man would then be a history of evils and misfortunes. This historicism is pessimistic. This pessimism, however, has as its counterpoint the optimism for the implications of the use of method for man and the world. When the method was applied, for Bacon the evils of original sin and the Fall would be overcome, man would discover the absolute epistemologically and such knowledge would lead him to social harmony:

> Through sin, man has lost the innocence and dominion of creatures. Both losses can be repaired, even in part, even in this life, the first with religion and with faith, the second with the arts and the sciences. For the divine curse did not render the creature irreparably rebellious; but by virtue of that diploma: You shall eat bread with the sweat of your forehead, by means of various labors (certainly not by disputes or by idle magical ceremonies), there

comes to man, from somewhere, the bread which is destined to the uses of human life.[186]

This is in tune with another facet of Puritanism (at least part of it): post-millennial eschatological optimism. This doctrine teaches that there will be, before the end of the world, a period where the faith of Christianity flourishes, similar to ideas about the Golden Age – logically, but with peculiar characteristics. The correct thing is that for post-millennial Puritans, there is optimism about the future through the concept of growth of the Christian faith in the world. 'Scientfying' this concept, he believes in a kind of millennial period of humanity, in which man will dominate nature through the inductive method. Another important figure in Baconian eschatology is that of the enemy, the adversary, theologically called the Antichrist. A significant number of Puritans saw the figure of the Antichrist in the papacy, which they believed, oppressed the true faith. In the field of science, Bacon saw the strong influence of Aristotelianism as a direct enemy of truth, which needed to be destroyed in order for the Millennial Age to occur. For him,

> There are three types of sources of errors and false philosophies: the sophistry, the empirical, and the superstitious. The most conspicuous example of the first is that of Aristotle.[187]

As stated earlier, Bacon's intellectual context was favorable to this criticism of Aristotle. His contemporary Thomas Hobbes (1588-1679) even called Aristotle an Antichrist. Both thinkers came to work together, and it is not difficult to imagine that Bacon knew of Hobbes' anti-Aristotelian spirit too. At any rate, for Bacon, the onset of progress was directly proportional to the decline of obscurantism. There would be no greater force contrary to his method in the final period of the Middle Ages, in spite of the growth of nominalism, for Bacon. Therefore, his criticism of him and the other ancient thinkers was not only an intellectual critique but, in a way, a political attitude, standing against what he believed to be obscurantism. However, his stance was not a politically open and revolutionary stance, covered

---

[186] BACON, Francis. *The Advancement of Learning* [1605], pp. 230-231.
[187] Ibid., p. 16.

by academic rhetoric. He was well aware that a substantial change in the field of politics would be impossible without first becoming aware of reality. Thus gnosis, once again, would be the basis of their millennialism, though they had ignored pessimism on the matter of the Gnostic dualism in the first centuries of Christianity. Such gnosis, once again, presents itself as a conjunction between Hermetic monism and heterodox Protestantism.

Bacon's criticism of Roman Catholicism, which with Aristotle's scholasticism and influence had denied induction, confused theology with philosophy, and privileged deduction and contemplation, is only one of the criticisms of thinkers influenced by humanism and skepticism, made in favor of secularization and disenchantment of the world and devoid of any religious rigor. This is not the case, however. The idea that was the 'sign of the times' that had permeated the minds of the reformers was also present in Bacon. Luther even thought that the world would not last long after his generation. The Zuinglians and proto-Calvinists, in general, owned the motto *Post Tenebras Lux*, in which the era of the reform would be an era of illumination that proceeded the era of Roman Catholic darkness. Some more enthusiastically thought that Luther was an angel of the apocalypse. The Anabaptist radical groups possessed certain millenarian factions, among them the idea that a prophet called himself King, like David, and taught the necessity of building the kingdom by the sword, since the historical moment in which they lived was the moment of the victory for divine help. These examples took place in Continental Europe. In England, in turn, there were neoadamists who, judging themselves to be pure as the Adam before the Fall, went barefoot since the moment of overcoming sin had come. In fact, these sectarians had resurrected—or made their own version of—a heretical movement called the *Spirit-Free Brothers*. Once again, the idea of liberation was present. Such a sense of liberation from morality was also present in the Ranters, who had not the slightest modesty about blaspheming the official faith and practicing a sensualism opposed to the asceticism of traditional Christianity.[188] The quest for overcoming and liberation

---

[188] "A compulsive desire to curse and blaspheme [...] [Had] dominated [a Ranter] in his youth, but he was able to withstand it for good twenty-seven years. Then,

from the Christian tradition that was associated with "peasant" and communist ideals was present among the Diggers and Levellers, who were considered to be prototypes of the modern English political left. All these groups were, to a certain extent, contemporaries of Bacon and, directly or indirectly, dealt with the religious conception of the world. Similarly, Bacon's criticism of Roman Catholicism is not a criticism of religion in general. Hegel (1770-1831) later criticized medieval Christianity while, in addition to being a self-proclaimed Lutheran, he saw Luther as the one who had brought light to the Germans, so for him Germany would not need the French Enlightenment. A similar appreciation of Luther was held by Goethe (1749-1832). What Bacon wanted was to prevent the revival of Catholic dominion over England, to restrain the reaction of the defenders of the Aristotelian-Thomist doctrine, of scholasticism, and of the subservice of academic or scientific work to the Holy See. With Protestantism, especially the less doctrinaire and more latitudinal type, the English philosopher saw a chance to undertake scientific work with greater independence from the religious institution—since Protestantism was institutionally less centralized than Catholicism—without negotiating its faith, since, for him, it would remain intact in a separate field of scientific inquiry.[189]

---

however, he tried to make up for lost time. I wanted to say, once, 'to hear a mighty angel (within the man) utter a delicious blasphemy, from those who come with their mouth full,' to hear the preaching of an orthodox minister." HILL, Christopher. *The World Upside Down: Radical Ideas During the English Revolution of 1640*. Trad. br. Renato Janine Ribeiro. São Paulo: Companhia das Letras, 1987, pp. 202-203.

[189] "Martin Luther, doubtless guided by a higher Providence, but reflecting on the enterprise which he had assumed before the Bishop of Rome and the degenerate traditions of the Church, and perceiving his own solitude, finding no help in the opinions of his time, he was obliged to awaken all antiquity and to call to his aid the past times to form a party against the present [...] And from this were born again a delight in his style and writing, and an admiration for this way of writing Thus the confluence of these four causes: the admiration of the ancient authors, hatred of the scholastics, the accurate study of languages, and the efficacy of predication, gave rise to an ardent study of the eloquence and ease of speech, which then began to bloom." BACON, Francis. *The Advancement of Learning* [1605], pp. 45-47.

3.6 Comparative Table Describing the Influence of Religion on Bacon

In order to facilitate the understanding of what has been said so far, it is illustrated in the table below:

TABLE 1:
A COMPARISON OF PROTESTANT DOCTRINES & THE SCIENCE OF BACON

	Doctrines of some Protestant Religious in the Sixteenth and Seventeenth centuries	Francis Bacon
Original Sin	Their evils could be braked, but never totally eliminated in this life.	Original sin could be eliminated in this life.
Revelation	Given supernaturally by God.	Given as by the absolutized super-reality or by the occult in nature.
Grace or Light	Transmitted by the Means of Grace: Preaching the Gospel and administering the Sacraments or just Preaching the Gospel.	Transmitted by true inductive method
Knowledge	Superior knowledge of reality is given through the Means of Grace.	Higher knowledge is a kind of liberating gnosis transmitted by method, a kind of Medium of Grace.
Eschatology	During a period of Christian growth post-millennialists create a type of Golden Age in the world through the Means of Grace.	There will be a period of growth of liberation against error (idols) and progress (a type of Golden Age) through the method, a kind of Medium of Grace.

3.7 The Influence of These Ideas on Bacon's Critique of the Ancients

The first chapter demonstrated the influence of Renaissance mysticism and, indirectly Neoplatonism, on Bacon. Thus, his criticism of the ancients was directed to the philosophy of Aristotle. In this chapter, the study of the Baconian critique of the ancients will be more comprehensive.

3.7.1 TRANSCENDENCE AND IMMANENCE: CRITICISM AND CONCESSION

Despite the interpretive divergences, it can be said that the classical interpretation of Plato and Aristotle views them as philosophers who, respectively, are characterized by a greater emphasis on transcendence and immanence. Plato's interpretation as a dualist makes him a defender of the realism of universals more sharply than Aristotle. Hence, the greater defense of the importance of numbers, mathematics, and geometry, which are crucial to the Platonic doctrine of universals and their concept of form. Aristotle, despite being opposed to monism and a pluralistic view of things, when interpreted as a moderate and more immanentist realist, is considered more "materialistic" (or biologist) than Plato.[190] For example, the Stagirite did not separate the study of movement from the study of things – for him there is no movement outside things. Also contributing to this understanding of Aristotelian doctrines about hylomorphism and knowledge, was his critique of the Pythagoreans and Plato's emphasis on numbers, as well as the critique of what he understood to be the platonic adherence of numbers as intermediaries between the sensible and the world of ideas, beyond his criticism of Plato's doctrine of forms. During the Catholic era, whether patristic or scholastic, transcendentalism

---

[190] "There is no movement out of things, for what changes always changes either substantially or quantitatively or qualitatively or locally, and, as we have said, there is nothing that is common to such changes and is not either an "it" or a quantity, or a quality or any of the other categories." ARISTOTLE, *Physics*. Guillermo R. de Echandia Translation, Editorial Gredos, Madrid, 1985, p. 177.

and immanentism were present in philosophical reflection, even if not as openly and directly as they were, according to interpreters, in Plato and Aristotle. The influence of Platonism and Stoicism were present in Philo of Alexandria (10-50), a Jew who influenced Christian doctrine, and to a certain extent, the Alexandrian Christian theologians, especially Origen (185-254). The famous Latin theologian Saint Augustine (354-430) was indebted to Platonic theology. It turns out that the Platonism that this author dealt with was, most of the time, the Neoplatonism of Plotinus, which gave Plato a monist interpretation. Thomistic Aristotelianism was, in turn, a watershed in Catholic theology. Aristotle became the philosopher *par excellence* of the West and overshadowed the legacy that Plato had possessed. What seems at first sight to be a philosophical rupture in Aquinas is shown to be a discontinuity, if one takes into account the conceptions of transcendence and immanence of Christian philosophy. In addition, Christian orthodoxy rejected the doctrine of reincarnation, affirmed the non-dualistic doctrine of incarnation, affirmed the personality of the divine, rejected the consideration of matter as evil, and defended the perpetuity of the resurrected body. This denotes that the Platonism of Orthodox Christians either interpreted Plato differently from the dualist thesis and purposely modified it to make it favorable to Christian doctrine, or drank strongly from Plotinian Neoplatonism. The possibility of these options being accepted together is also valid. Thus, Aristotelianism, redeemed in its prestige (or greater prestige) by Muslim Arabs and made sovereign by Aquino, did not necessarily have to be considered antagonistic to this Christian Platonism.

Bacon seems to consider Plato a mere deductivist and puts him in opposition to the pre-Socratic empiricist philosophers. This is one of the factors why Bacon has been considered an anti-platonic.[191] However, it is necessary to consider the fact that Bacon's conception of Plato's philosophy did not imply a rejection of the same degree of "Christian Platonism" set forth above. Considering that Plotinian Neoplatonism does not have the dualism seen by Bacon in Plato, it would not be incorrect to say that between Plato's Baconian

---

[191] BACON, Francis. *The Advancement of Learning* [1605], p. 148.

interpretation as a mere deductivist, Plotinian Neoplatonism, and his criticism of Aristotle, the school which may have had some influence is the second. As stated in the previous chapter, Hermetic monism, which was also influenced by Plotinian and Neoplatonic thinking, had a certain influence on Bacon's worldview. The Plato of Christianity or Neoplatonism is the subject of this critique of deductivism because deductive logic, for the English philosopher, anticipates empiria with abstract ideas and affirms the existence of transcendent entities and substances that could not be experienced by the inductive method – by inference, they should be categorized as more like immanentism. This Renaissance Platonism is less dualistic than Plato's own ordinary interpretation, and becomes, with his ideas, more eager for empathy and immanence, and can be partially accepted by Bacon. More than that, because the Neoplatonism of certain Renaissance writers is more monistic, "Plato," which Bacon considered a "man endowed with high ingenuity," may be more compatible with Bacon's thinking than Aristotle. He affirmed that there are truths to be preserved in the ancient authors.[192]

What does this mean? Three things: Firstly, that Bacon preferred immanentism to the transcendentalist view of the world, even if he did not reduce his ideas to one of them. Immanenism is more empirical. But, as Bacon never showed himself to be a disciple of any school, it was unclear in his actions and words. He was more immanenist-empiricist than Plato (he thought) was, and even criticized these Platonic ideas. Also, with the pre-Socratic philosophy superseded by later philosophy, in combination with the concept of progress, it is impracticable to define succinctly. Secondly, it is well known that Bacon was an opponent of Aristotelian immanenism-empiricism and what he considered to be Platonic deductivism. Because these two philosophers had exerted a strong influence on practically all western thought until his time, Bacon became erroneously known by some as a mere denier of the philosophy of the ancients. This error is shown by the fact that Bacon was influenced by the Neoplatonic mysticism of the Renaissance Hermeticists. Thus, in the third place, Bacon provided continuity for some of the philosophical ideas that preceded it. To know the degree of influence of Neoplatonism on

---

[192] Ibid., p. 145.

Bacon is not the purpose of this investigation, but rather to show that Bacon does not have absolutely new ideas (that break with the whole history of philosophy), but defends progress and the idea of the new.

Moreover, if Aristotle is directly attacked by him, at least Plato was preserved by Christians, even the Protestants, and Plato was revered in the Renaissance. Bacon was not considered as an Antichrist, as Aristotle was,[193] and could be partly accepted – but also argued with. Such ideas as the unity of the real, which was in Bacon under the rhetoric of the unifying order of nature—without whose knowledge it would be impossible to unify all empirical data to arrive at a unified knowledge of the absolute, the fundamental function of numbers in the whole of reality—was in Bacon in the concept that the knowledge acquired after the end of the whole empirical process would be a mathematical knowledge of reality, and the way in which it was concealed in matter. Bacon had the idea that absolute knowledge was at the end of the complete study of nature, as if behind it or hidden in it.

3.7.2 RESPONSES TO PLATONIC DUALISM AND TO THE REALISTIC INTERPRETATION OF ARISTOTELIAN PHILOSOPHY

Both Aristotle, the mid-Platonics, and Neoplatonics interpreted Plato as a philosopher whose ideas were not systematically and definitely given in the text. For Aristotle, by way of example, Plato considered numbers as intermediates between the material world and the ideal world par excellence. Thus, mathematical knowledge in Plato, according to Aristotle, was not a mere knowledge of material

---

[193] "The initial 'guilt' of the Greeks, who produced a philosophy incapable of procreation, was added to [Bacon] a second, even more serious fault: the moderns entrusted and entrusted their fate to that sterile philosophy, they replaced the cult of nature, which is the work of God, by the cult of some ancient philosophers. To this idolatrous attitude corresponds a renunciation of the faculties that God has granted to men. When one takes into account the ground on which this condemnation is born and fed, it is not surprising that the figure of Aristotle and that of the Antichrist are close." ROSSI, Paolo. *The Science and Philosophy of the Modern*. Trad. br. Álvaro Lorencini. São Paulo: UNESP, 1992, p. 66.

entities, but of entities whose references were not themselves, such as pure ideas, nor matter, since numbers would not be forms of material elements.

Gnostics in the early centuries of Christianity used Platonic concepts to lead them to an esoteric truth that only the initiates could know and convey. Plato's successor in his Academy, Speusippus (408-339 BC), is an important source for such an assimilation of esotericism in Plato. Plotinus' Neoplatonism said that the knowledge of the One was not due to the superficial knowledge of things, neither by what is said about things, but by the enlightening knowledge that intuits transcendence which is not reducible to a simple categorization, that is, it would reach knowledge of the One behind the human conception of One. Plotinus' ideas, coupled with the apophatic theology of Dionysius the Areopagite, said that the knowledge of God is a negative knowledge – by the negation of limiting things one arrives at the limitless which is not reducible to language. *Theosis* by Gregory Palamas (1296-1359) also relates that the enlightened man must unite with the divine by asceticism, which formed the basis of theology for the Orthodox Church. The Renaissance, in general, created a synthesis between Hermeticism and Neoplatonism and continued to defend the esoteric aspect of Platonic philosophy. Here it is believed that it was with the already modern, anti-mystical, and rationalist mentality typical of more progressive followings of German Protestantism that a marked criticism began of Plato's esoteric interpretation, which was present in the greatest Platonic traditions throughout history. Tenneman (1761-1819), and especially Scheliermacher (1798-1834), who is considered the father of liberal or revisionist-progressive theology, are examples of this mentality. This type of Protestantism, drawing on the Sola Scriptura tradition, drew a hermeneutic view that the Hermeneut should have as his office the study of the text and not speculation on what the text itself had not shown. Scholars like E. R. Dodds (1893-1979), Johann Bucker (1696-1770), Harold F. Cherniss (1904-1887), and Gregory Vlastos (1907-1991) sought to show, from the studies of the Platonic texts themselves, that the mid-platonic theses and the Neoplatonic are both deviations from the original Platonism or criticize Aristotle and the later Platonists had misrepresented Plato. These ideas were in turn attacked by E. N. Tigerstedt (1907-1979), Charles Kahn, and Leo Catana.

In the twentieth century, a school offered new insights, and a return to Plato's esoteric-mystical interpretation, namely the School of Tübingen. Authors such as Hans Gaiser, Joachim Krämer, Kenneth Sayre, and Findlay have reinstated Plato's perspective as a thinker whose teachings transcend the textual structure itself, thus possessing an esoteric character. This study agrees with the School of Tübingen for some important reasons, including the following facts:

1. Although not logically impossible, it is statistically and rationally improbable that virtually all the immediate disciples of Plato and his followers over the centuries, who were closest to his person, language, and culture, were wrong about the mystical and mysterious nature of his thought.

2. Platonic writings are not systematic but speculative. Therefore, grammatical information does not systematize the ontological truth that is signaled by the linguistic sign. It is, therefore, necessary to understand the information transmitted, to go beyond the grammatical and to enter into other spheres, such as the aesthetics of geometric figures and numerical signs, etc.

3. The Platonic concept of the intelligible world, by logical inference, prevents such an intelligible world from being ontologically described by the sound of words, which is associated with the physical entity of the vocal cords, and the visible or physical sign of words, geometric forms or written numbers. Therefore, language, when it speaks of the intelligible world, must be, for Plato, a symbol of a reality that it cannot reduce to its sphere.

4. The School of Tübingen is not just one school, among others. Its defenders are equivalent to a great part of the interpreters of Plato during the centuries. Their theses are not new. The denial of mysticism or esotericism in Plato is a modern novelty, while the School of Tübingen is in tune with most of Plato's interpreters throughout history.

If these theses are correct and Plato points to a supralinguistic reality which, through language, can only be described symbolically and allegorically, not only Plato's dualism is questioned but also the realistic interpretation of Aristotle. How does this happen? If the intelligible world is so transcendent that it cannot even be ontologically expressed and understood, what exists is a problem in which the immanent world does not exist. It is inferred that the sensible world can be considered it's opposite as if both are in themselves or are not known in themselves, but only as a function of transcendence. Thus, Plato would best be described as an idealist monist. Aristotle, in his turn, in criticizing Plato, was not opposed to dualism, but to a monism. Moreover, in defending hylomorphism, Aristotle would not be denying a separation of form and substance from Plato, but rather the way to achieve this harmonious separation, which he himself made. Therefore, it would not represent a tradition that reduced the knowledge of ontological substance to language.[194]

If intermediate forms and numbers do not exist in Aristotle, and yet form is not reduced to material substance, but at the same time matter, being subject to time, cannot be classified as being exactly the same, nor subject to time and pure act, it is reasonable to question whether the concepts of act and substance for material elements are no more pedagogical and rhetorical than ontological and whether there is in practice an approximation of Aristotle to non-realism. Interpretations suspecting a kind of anti-realism in Aristotle are present in Martha Nussbaum,[195] who sees it as a kind of internal realism, and in Lloyd, Lacey, and Harter,[196] for whom Aristotle is closer to nominalism or conceptualist non-realism than realism.[197]

---

[194] DAVIDSON, Jack. *Philosophical Studies: An International Journal for Philosophy in the Analytic Tradition*, Vol. 63, No. 2 (Aug., 1991), USA, pp. 147-166.

[195] NEWTON, Joseph. *Triad: Critique of Dualism, Support of Monism in Plato.* Valdosta State University, June, USA, 1992.

[196] TERENCE, Irwin. *Aristotle's First Principles.* Claredon Paperbacks. New York: Oxford University, 1988.

[197] According to Corrigan: "A school of thought maintains that Aristotle posits a first common and underlying matter to the elements (Solmsen, Robinson, Dancy). Another school denies that he does not do so (King, Charlton, Jones) [...] Thus, according to a third view, Aristotle postulates a matter common to

If these questions are valid, if it is possible to conceive of Plato as a monistic mystic[198] and Aristotle as a kind of nominalist, conceptualist nonrealist, or internal realist, then Bacon is not so contrary to those influences. In other words, if this perspective is taken into account in Plato,[199] in either Aristotle's or Bacon's criticism, neither of

the elements, but this would not be a matter, if understood as a mere substrate (Cohen) [...] A fourth interpretation holds that [...] the first matter (the substrate of the celestial world) [is] minimally determined [...] [by] a principle – matter completely indeterminate (Happ). Finally, according to a recent interpretation, the elements are not composed, but simple bodies that serve as matter for each other. There is no need, therefore, for a [first] matter ... other than the elements (Gill)." CORRIGAN, Kevin, *Plotinus' Theory of Matter-Evil and the Question of Substance: Plato, Aristotle, and Alexander of Aphrodisias*. Leuven: Peeters, 1995, p. 97.

[198] "The relation between the constitution between the world and the four elements in the *Timaeus* can give way to a more monist interpretation of Plato: Thus the constitution of the world took each of these four elements in their totality. It was from the totality of fire, water, air, and earth that the one who constituted the world constituted it, leaving no part or property whatever, for this was his design: first, that it was above of everything, a complete and perfect living being, constituted from perfect parts; then it would be unique, since there would be nothing left from which another of the same nature could be generated; and that he was immune to aging and disease, for he was perfectly aware that heat, cold, and other violent forces, surrounding a compound body and falling on it, dissolve it and, imposing disease and causes them to be destroyed. It was for this reason, and based on this reasoning, that from the globality of all produced a single perfect whole, immune to aging and disease." See *Timaeus-Critias*. Trad. br. Rodolfo Lopes. Coimbra: CECH, 2011, pp.101-10.

[199] Plato's anthropological concept, whose existence of the masculine and feminine gender is due to the original androgyne, can also give way to a more immanenistic interpretation of the origin of things in Plato: "Androgynous was then a distinct genus, both in form in the common name of the two, the masculine and the feminine, while now it is nothing more than a name put on dishonor. Then, a whole was the form of each man, with the rounded back, the flanks in a circle; four hands he had, and his legs the same so much of the hands, two faces upon a turning neck, similar in all; but the head on the two faces opposite each other was one, and four ears, two sexes, and everything else as these examples could be assumed. And as for his walk, he was as erect as he is now, in either direction he wanted; but when they launched themselves into a rapid rush, as those who tumbling and turning their legs up make a wheel, likewise, leaning on their eight limbs of then, they quickly circled. That is why there were three genders, and such was their constitution, for the masculine at the beginning was descended from the sun, the feminine from the earth, and what was of the two was from the moon;

them contains criticism of thinkers who opposed empiricism. The criticism would be, in fact, the way they treated empiria. Thus, if one studies all his works and his deeper intentions, it is reasonable to defend a certain continuity between Plato, Aristotle, and Bacon as to the central purpose of philosophy: the knowledge of a non-dualistic or non-unnatural reality. Discontinuity is not, according to this interpretation, in the very essence of its philosophies, which are all experimental, but only in secondary matter, since it is only in the way that the experiences are transformed into method in each of these thinkers differ.

3.7.3 ARISTOTLE AND DEMOCRITUS

Bacon said that Democritus (460-370 BC) was superior to Plato and Aristotle. He added that together with Leucippus, Democritus had developed a conception of a vacuum superior to that of Aristotle.[200] However, with the claim that "the school of Democritus [...] more than others penetrated the secrets of nature,"[201] did he mean to say that he agreed with Democritean atomism? No. This statement was aimed at a different purpose: to criticize the later philosophy of Socrates for the anthropocentric turn and to show that the pre-Socratics, especially Democritus, according to Bacon, were more aware that empirical philosophy was the only one that would enable knowledge objective of reality. It turns out that Bacon read Plato with the preconception of his dualism, thus considering him a mere deductivist, and read Aristotle[202] with the preconceptions about his logic and the empirical study of reality. The use of this statement by

---

and they were thus circular, both themselves and their locomotion, because they had similar parents." PLATO. *The Banquet*. Pará de Minas: Acropolis Version, 2003, p. 20.

[200] Democritus had affirmed that man is formed of a tessitura of atoms of body and of atoms of spirit, alternating one by one ... See DA SILVA apud LUCRÉCIO. *From Nature*. Trad. br. Agostinho da Silva. São Paulo: Abril Cultural, 1980, p. 68.

[201] BACON, Francis. *Novum Organum* [1620], p. 32.

[202] Aristotle said that "Democritus, for his part, denies that the first bodies have begotten each other; for him the common body is the beginning of all things, differentiating them in magnitude and figure." See ARISTOTLE. *Physics*, p. 190.

Bacon on Democritus has some implications, including the facts that:

1. Bacon's interpretation of Plato and Aristotle does not seem to have been fully correct.
2. In a peculiar way, not removed from Democritus, Bacon subconsciously uses religious categories in his ideas, which makes him resemble Pythagorean and Platonic mysticism in this matter.
3. The atomism of Democritus and Leucippus can be synthesized with a heterodox use of Platonic and Aristotelian philosophies, which the syncretic and contradictory practice of Bacon's thought seems to have done.
4. Even the pre-Socratics are superstitious, for Bacon. Aristotle's error would be less a mistake of superstition than a misuse of more sophisticated logic.
5. The influence of Democritus on the Renaissance mystics and on Protestant Christians who, in turn, influenced Bacon, is much smaller than the influence exerted on them by Plato and Aristotle.

It is, therefore, necessary to conclude that if there is any continuity between the tradition of Democritus and the tradition of Bacon, this fact does not negate the argument that there is also some continuity between Platonism, Aristotelianism, and Baconianism.[203]

---

[203] "Bacon, as we know, contrasted with the philosophy of Plato and of Aristotle the oldest natural philosophers. In the homeomeries of Anaxagoras, in the atoms of Leucippus and Democritus, in the sky and in the land of Parmenides, in the discord and friendship of Empedocles, in the fire of Heraclitus, is there a "taste of natural philosophy, of the nature of things, of experience, of bodies" (*Novum Organum*, I, 63) that was lost when philosophy turned itself to the inner world instead of nature, to problems of moral and linguistic character, abandoning the severe research of natural things. Aristotle tried to erase the memory of his predecessors, but it is not true that the works of the ancient philosophers were immediately forgotten after he triumphed over them by virtue of his authority." See ROSSI, Paolo. *Shipwrecks without Spectators: The Idea of Progress*. Trad. br. Álvaro Lorencini. São Paulo, UNESP, 2000, pp. 26-27.

3.7.4 BACON:
NEITHER OPPOSED TO PLATO NOR CONTRARY TO ARISTOTLE

After the study of evidence and possibilities, this chapter concludes with the defense of some theses:

1. Even if Bacon's interpretation of Plato and Aristotle is considered correct, it is possible to affirm that he was influenced by Neoplatonism. And, indirectly, by Aristotelianism itself, since Neoplatonism is not at all antagonistic to Aristotelianism.

2. If interpretations of Plato and Aristotle as alternatives to the hegemonic are considered, Bacon can still be considered closer to Plato and Aristotle, because the criticism of Bacon to Plato, Aristotle, and the pre-Socratics is not an absolute rejection of their ideas.

3. The function of Christianity in the reinterpretation of Plato and Aristotle is fundamental to understand Bacon's relationship with these Greek authors. Protestant Christianity, in particular, was fundamental to Bacon, for it eliminates the more speculative aspects of Platonism and Aristotelianism within Roman Catholicism.

4. Protestant Christianity, being more practical and less contemplative or speculative than medieval Christianity, was a key element in understanding Bacon's use of both transcendence and immanence since it is less speculative than scholasticism and more open to the empirical – without proposing to stop regarding the transcendent.

5. Bacon did treat the transcendent as the patristic theologians, influenced by Plato and the scholastic theologians, did. However, influenced by Protestantism, one cannot, even subconsciously, exclude the transcendent from research.

6. Bacon's empirical work, like Aristotle's, did not reduce reality to matter. But this occurs in a way that is philosophically distinct from Aristotle and in a theologically heterodox manner.

In short, Bacon was empirical, but not materialistic; he dealt with the transcendent, but without being idealistic; he was mystical, but also a logical (inductivist); he was contrary to the ancients, but also a continuation of their work; he criticized religion, but synthesized into his thinking various elements from the new Christian groups in England, including Protestantism. It is in this context that Bacon must be understood when one is to study his criticism of the ancients, especially Plato, Aristotle, and their influence on Christianity. However, a better understanding of the Baconian inductive method itself will be the target of the next chapter's investigation.

4.

THE INDUCTIVE METHOD OF BACON: ITS STRUCTURE AND COMPLEXITY

UNLIKE THE FIRST TWO CHAPTERS, WHICH FOCUSED ON THE mystical and religious aspect of Bacon, this chapter focuses on the inductive method itself. This is necessary because the understanding of the Baconian method will ensure that in the fourth chapter, mysticism, religiosity, and the inductive method are considered together and discussed with modern and contemporary science. The first section will introduce the Baconian inductive method. The second section will study the Tables of Presence, Absence, and Comparison. The subsection will investigate the Baconian concept of act law. The third section will investigate the thesis of Bacon's epistemological naivety. The fourth section will seek to understand *technés* meaning in Bacon. The fifth section, in turn, will study the relationship between induction and ethics in thinking. The sixth section will investigate the scientific neutrality of techné in Bacon. The seventh section will explain Bacon's importance to the Royal Society and the connection between Baconian induction and politics. The eighth section will attempt to expose the differences and similarities between the General Systems Theory, Epistemology of Systems Thinking, and Bacon's thinking. The ninth section will summarize the nine sections that preceded it. The tenth and final section will briefly present the real causes of Bacon's critique of the ancients and especially of Aristotle.

4.1 The Inductive Method Itself: Introductory Questions

Bacon's inductive method proposed to be a watershed moment in scientific activity.[204] He related his method to the concept as "new" with the idea that it was an "opening" in history, beginning a new phase of the world, which, being subjected to the study of reality by this method, would lead man to progress. Bacon did not deny that he had seen wisdom in the world before him. He wrote a book about it: *The Wisdom of the Ancients*. Nor did he deny that there was induction in the science of the past. Despite these points of contact with his method and the science that preceded it, Bacon did not moderate his rhetoric concerning "progress" and "new." How was this possible? To the English philosopher, the discourse on the legacy of the ancients did not imply that this legacy had influenced its method. Bacon treated his inductive method as if it were an "a-historical" entity. For example, when he admitted that there had been some induction in the past, he did not pay the same attention to the fact that his method was not entirely new. If the initial premise is that induction, even if incomplete, has already been applied in the past, it cannot be concluded that the induction now proposed is qualitatively different from its predecessors. As an induction, possessing characteristics common to the other studies also referred to as "inductive," it must submit to the whole that characterizes all "inductions," that is, what all these "inductions" have in common. This precludes the idea that "absolutely new induction" is real, intelligible, and verifiable. Moreover, the idea of progress in the absolute sense becomes impracticable, because if induction itself is related to this progress, any use of induction in the past, even if it has been a limited use, somehow "participates" in it. Indeed, the progress that Bacon intended should "preserve" something (and this would already be a tradition) of the progress bequeathed by "imperfect"

---

[204] On his method, Bacon says, "Even if the mills of all time were to be assembled, combined, and combined, great progress would not be made in the sciences through anticipations, for the radical errors perpetrated in the mind, in the first disposition, would not be cured for the excellence of the operations nor for the subsequent remedies." BACON, Francis. *Novum Organum* [1620], p. 19.

inductivists of the past. In a concrete sense, the "new" and "progress" related to the Baconian induction can only be considered "new" and "progress" quantitatively. The induction of Bacon sums up the characteristics present in the set of induction's own aspects, which are agents of the process of differentiation. But that does not happen at all. Differentiation does not exclude similarities. The quantitative difference does not exclude qualitative equality. So, there are some basic truths to recognize in order to better understand Bacon's design of his inductive method:

1. Bacon believed that his inductive method was absolutely new and contradicted, to a certain extent, himself as to the wisdom of the ancient inductivists or,

2. Either consciously or unconsciously used the concept of "new" more as political rhetoric than in a literal sense – as if the "new" was a category of thought linked to a real entity.

3. In any case, contradictory or rhetorical, there was in Bacon an external influence on the elaboration of his inductive method.

4. The Baconian inductive method itself is therefore not neutral in research and or infallible epistemologically and must be treated not only as an object of the history of technique but in view of its historical, political, and mystical conjuncture.

After this explanation, we shall proceed to study some details of the Baconian inductive method itself.

4.2 *The Question of the Functionality of Method: Tables of Presence, Absence, and Comparison*

Bacon stated in the *Novum Organum*, published as a counterpoint to the Aristotelian Organ, that his inductive method operated using the *Tables of Presence, Absence, and Comparison*, for "the purpose and office of these three tables is to make a *summons before the intellect* [...] once the quotation is made, it is necessary to proceed to the practice of induction." For him, the use of the three tablets allows his inductive method to be practiced without the errors of the inductivism that preceded it. After the study of the tablets comes the first vintage and the *experimentalum crucis*, capable of assuring the plausibility of one hypothesis and rendering obsolete the others. The old inductivists,[205] according to Bacon, anticipated theoretical and deductive prejudices, thus preventing truly satisfactory results from arising. Aristotle and other early inductivists jumped from particular utterances to general statements without the scrutiny of precise empirical inquiry. Bacon tried to correct this error by stating that it was necessary for the inductivist to begin with the particular utterances, to continue with the intermediate statements, to arrive at the general statements. Thus, the Baconian inductive method presents itself as the one that avoids these anticipations and prejudices. Hence the necessity of the tablets.

In the first table, according to Bacon, a *quotation* must be made before the intellect of all known instances, which agree with the same nature, even if they are found in dissimilar matters.[206] For this purpose, the nature of heat and its residence in dissimilar materials were studied. Among the various cited examples where heat remains in different instances, Bacon mentions the "eruptions of flames from the craters of the hills" in example number five, "natural hot baths" in example number eight, and "heated hot liquids" in example number nine. The English philosopher was sure that this table had proved that in all these instances the phenomenon of heat occurred and that all these materials—water, mounds, craters, etc.—had something in common: heat. The utility and accuracy of the presence table could then be proven. The second board, in turn, the "Table of Deviance (or Declination) or of Absence in Near Phenomena,"[207] should list the similar instances in which a given nature is absent.

---

[205] In criticizing other models of induction, Bacon says: "The induction that proceeds by simple enumeration is puerile, leads to precarious conclusions, exposes itself to the danger of an instance that contradicts it [...] But induction which will be useful for the discovery and demonstration of the sciences and of the arts must analyze the nature, proceeding to the due rejections and exclusions, and then, in possession of the necessary negative cases, conclude on the positive cases." Ibid., p. 69.

[206] Ibid., pp. 95-96.

[207] Ibid., p. 104.

Bacon clarifies the work of the second board with the following example: "The rays of the moon, the stars, and the comets do not bring warmth to the touch, but on the contrary, it is at the fullest extent that the coldest rigors are observed."[208] In such cases a limit may be placed on the "recall of positive and negative instances"[209] by adding to the first table, which deals with the (positive) presence of one nature in different instances, and the limits of the same nature by verifying the absence (denial) of that nature in other instances.[210] Finally, the third board, the "Table of Degrees or Comparison",[211] is a kind of middle ground or intermediate board between the tables of presence and absence, since it does not deal with the presences and absences themselves, but rather the degrees of presence and absences of a nature manifested in the same object or in "diverse objects."[212] In this we know not only the variation of the presence and absence of a nature in the same object or in different objects, but also the knowledge of the variation of the forms in these same instances, since in Bacon nature and form are inseparable and that for him, "One cannot take nature by true form unless it always decreases when that nature descends and likewise always increases as nature increases."[213] Bacon uses examples of such a table, among others, the lack of equality of cold in wood and metal, the preservation of heat in "equine manure, or lime, or perhaps ashes, or soot caused by fire"[214] and heat variation between larger and smaller animals, such as insects, and the influence of the tropical climate on this. With the three boards, according to Bacon, inductive method is apt to investigate nature.

---

[208] Ibid., p. 104.

[209] Ibid., p. 105.

[210] The similarity of this Baconian idea to Corrigan's interpretation of the concept of matter in Aristotle is interesting. According to him, Corrigan says that "Aristotle and Alexander [of Aphrodysias] distinguish the deprivation of matter. Deprivation is contrary to form, not matter." CORRIGAN, Kevin. *Plotinus's Theory of Matter-Evil and the Question of Substance: Plato, Aristotle, and Alexander of Aphrodisias*, p. 64.

[211] BACON, Francis. *Novum Organum* [1620], p. 114.

[212] See MAGEE, Bryan. *Popper's Ideas*, pp. 39-41.

[213] BACON, Francis. *Novum Organum*, p. 114.

[214] Ibid., p. 114.

In the true inductive method, according to Bacon, there must first be the "rejection or exclusion of the singular natures"[215] – either when "they are not found in any instance where the given nature is present,"[216] or "are in any instance in the given nature is not present,"[217] and when "they grow in any instance in whose given nature it decreases or decreases when the given nature grows."[218] In his *History of the Winds*, to have a practical idea, Bacon proposed the "Table of Human Requirements with reference to the Winds."[219] It is only after this process of rejection and exclusion that, according to him, one must begin to make affirmations and defend scientific hypotheses, since the form of nature was separated from instances that are strange or heterogeneous, for safety and objectivity in scientific research. But even the stage of hypothesis formulation is problematic in Bacon, since a "hypothesis," viewed as differing from "fact," is not actually nature itself, but a (hypothetical) human thesis about the natural world. Baconian statements about science, in order not to succumb to the same accusations made to Aristotle, for example, should be limited to concrete facts, not possibilities. The predictions of a Baconian scientific theory (hypothesis) should be like a factual prediction of the future, to be consistent with its criticism of ancient science. But the impasse between what is said and what is done continues.

4.2.1 THE FORMS AND LAW OF THE ACT

The search for forms is especially important for ancient philosophy, medieval philosophy—be it Christian, Jewish, or Islamic—and for Renaissance philosophy. All are influenced in a more or less accentuated way by Neoplatonic and Aristotelian metaphysics. Added to this was the preoccupation with the problem of movement and its relation to the idea of the immutable Being, eternal,

---

[215] Ibid., p. 116.
[216] Ibid., p. 123.
[217] Ibid., p. 123.
[218] BACON, Francis. *Novum Organum*, p. 123.
[219] BACON, Francis. *The Works of Francis Bacon Vol. 5: Translations of the Philosophical Works 2*. Edited by Spedding, Ellis, Heath. New York: Cambridge University Press, 2011, p. 198.

incorruptible, and intelligible, among other attributes. Aristotle, for example, explained the difference between motion and immutability with the idea of act and power. For him, power is changeable, and the act is related to the unchanging, the immobile. A baby is a potential adult and a child in the act. A small *Cupania Vernalis* is a tree in potency and a seed in act. The Pure Act, in turn, is what Aristotle appointed as the First Immovable Being. The fact that Aristotelians considered things by the union of matter (ὕλη) and form (μορφή) did not make them incapable of distinguishing them in any way, for, although united in the constitution of things (*synolo*), they understood that matter and form are differentiated principles: matter can take various forms and being associated with power and form being, as in the case of wood, which can take the forms of table, chair, door, etc. While a chair made of this wood would be the form that this particular matter (the wood) assumes in act.

It is not as difficult to understand the above as it is to understand[220] Bacon's use of the idea of an act. Oliveira, for example, argues that the English philosopher not only conceived of the distinction between form and matter in a similar way to Aristotle, but also understood the forms as being the microscopic parts of the phenomena in motion. Oliveira states:

> The confusing treatment that Bacon reserves for him (favored form) favored this term to be interpreted, either as an efficient cause or as a formal substance (which for many scholars would attest to the Aristotelian remnant), now as essence and now as general axioms, structural laws of matter, the movement of matter, fundamentals or principles. We believe, however, that it does not coincide with any of these concepts since the search for form is explicitly linked to the capacity for reproduction and transformation. Be that as it may, Bacon abandons conception as an entity, as in Aristotle, and outlines it as a combination of material units and movements, as intrinsic agents in the constitution of matter, thus paving the way for a mechanical or materialist explanation of the natural world. The knowledge of forms is the true knowledge of nature, which concerns the

---

[220] See pp. 95-96.

arrangement and movement of the microscopic parts of bodies, which can account for their natural appearances.[221]

If Aristotle rejected—due to his dualistic interpretation of Plato—what he considered to be a separation between matter and form in Platonic thought and tended towards a monistic unity between them, the difficulty of not mixing matter and form is even greater in Bacon, as has already been stressed. Bacon made no distinction between the two. He criticized Aristotle's use of the idea of power as an act to explain the density of air,[222] as well as the errors such as "to form the world on the basis of categories" and to be "more solicitous in formulating answers and presenting something positive in words than the inner truth of things." Bacon spoke of a *latent process* in treating dynamism of the phenomena and referring to a *latent schematic* – the internal structure of the phenomena. While critical, he did not vehemently reject the theory of Aristotelian causes, namely, the material, formal, efficient, and final causes. But the difficulty of synthesizing the barriers between what he said and the logic of his method remains.

Contrasting his doctrine of the act with that of the Aristotelian, Bacon called the Law of the Act "movement" since, according to him, it is only in coming to be that the act can be found. Hence, it could be said that there is only meaning in the idea of forms if they are the very laws of the act. How do we understand this? One possible explanation—which is not conclusive on the subject—is that the English philosopher wanted, by granting to the dynamics of inductive labor the status of a condition of the possibility of knowledge, to reveal the impossibility of Aristotle conceiving the act without the correct induction, and at the same time, to show that the true act is beyond the theoretical concept of the act. In order to know its law—which is the understood movement not as the Heraclitean becoming but as dynamic (δυναμις)—the necessity is to submit theory to practice. The inductive method then, preceding

---

[221] OLIVEIRA, Bernardo Jefferson de. *Francis Bacon and the Foundations of Science as Technology*, pp. 198-199.

[222] See BACON, Francis. *Novum Organum*, p. 32.

the theory, would find the form or law of the act at the end of the inductive process, which could make the very meaning of the words "form" and "act" modified by the paradigm acquired in the discovery of the new empirical facts.

4.2.2 THE PROBLEM OF INTERMEDIARIES AND REALISM

Certainly, Bacon could not reduce old science to the category of being "deductive." He recognized the presence of an induction among ancient thinkers. He even spoke of Aristotelian induction. What he could not grant was that they treat this induction as real or actual *induction*. The English philosopher argued that it was impossible for the old induction to be considered a true inducement[223] because its proponents fell into the same error as the deductivists: the use of theoretical anticipations preconceived to the detriment of the empiria itself. They lacked what Bacon considered to be the middle stage of the inductive process. It was precisely the intermediary phase of the process that would prevent the inductivist from jumping from the initial phase to the final stage without the necessary empirical evidence – thus erring in camouflaging these absences from data with theories not taken from nature. The inductive method proposed by Bacon should solve this problem. In it, the scientist should begin the empirical process with the so-called initial axioms, then move to the intermediate axioms, only to arrive at the final axioms. The intermediate axioms would then be a visible sign of a rupture between the Baconian induction and the induction of those who preceded it. Even though it is known that Aristotle used concepts as "average term" for his logic, this was not enough to avoid theoretical anticipations and constitute a truly empirical approach, subject to evidence in all its parts – initial, intermediate, and final. A practical example of these anticipations is found in the Aristotelian division of the sublunar and lunar worlds.[224] How could Aristotle conceive that the lunar world was more perfect, so

---

[223] BACON, Francis. *The Advancement of Learning* [1605], p. 136.

[224] Aristotle understood that the supralunar world was superior to the sublunary world. KEMPER, Érico. *The Insertion of Astronomy Topics in the Study of Mechanics in an Epistemological Approach*. Texts supporting the physics teacher v. 18 n. 3, Institute of Physics-UFRGS, 2007, Rio Grande do Sul, p. 8.

to speak than the sublunar world so that this statement was based on empirical evidence and not on theoretical conjectures? Bacon, save in his contradictions, sought to reject ideas that could not pass through the sieve of his method. In theory, therefore, intermediaries were used to prevent human curiosity from making its speculations and preconceptions into logically reasonable empirical facts.

Is Karl Popper's criticism (1902-1994) of what he considered naive in scientific work to be applied to Bacon? As a defender of falsification, the idea that a thesis is scientific when it presents potential falsifiers, which indicate a situation that makes it false. Popper, accusing inductivists as being naive about empirical work, seems to believe that they proposed a science whose theses corresponded to the facts in nature and that such theses would never be overcome. For Popper, scientific knowledge is a "hypothesis" about the regularity of certain phenomena that can be left aside when the facts falsify. But, for those whom Popper considers naive, science would not formulate only theses, but would describe the world as it is, unveiling nature—and if Kantian language is used—by knowing the phenomenon of the phenomenon itself. Earlier, this book provided reasons for Popper's view[225] of this naivete. Bacon had great ambitions for his inductive method, he believed that the *Instauratio Magna* would forever change the world through knowledge of the truth, and that induction and social progress were interconnected.[226] But this term, naivete, applied to pre-modern scientists by the moderns, should not be used without taking into account the preconceived circumstances surrounding modern science itself, among which are (1) the mechanical view of the world, (2) the conception of the world influenced by what Max Weber called disenchantment – which can also be called de-sacralization, 3) the context of the industrial revolution, the creation of machines—which is at the root of the contemporary robotic world—and 4) pragmatism related to individualism – which is also at the root of the contemporary globalized world. Bacon's contradictions, whether they are the result of a conscious but non-systematic activity or even

---

[225] BACON, Francis. *Novum Organum* [1620], pp. 30-35.
[226] POPPER, Karl. *Conjectures and Refutations*, pp. 45-46.

a subconscious one, do not reflect the inferiority of the author in relation to the scientists of his day and to those who preceded him. Whether scientists are still incapable of this today is another matter. The English philosopher, then, did not ultimately reduce knowledge to empirical data, nor did he reduce reality itself to perceptible phenomena, as has been shown by the study of the paradoxes in his thought. Wheeler argues that the science of Baconian administrative induction, as defended in the *Novum Organum*, deals more with "numeral things" than with realism and that the idea of Law by Bacon adopted is equivalent to form.[227] In fact, Lord Verulam, like other pre-modern scientists, was characterized by mysticism in science, whether he wanted to be or not. More pre-modern scientists who have not yet been directly attacked with the adjective "naïve" are now categorized as such—either to a greater or lesser degree—and Bacon should not have his work depreciated by that title either. Added to this is the fact that modern science and even Popperian falsificationism—already criticized by A. F. Chalmers (1939) and Paul Feyerabend (1924-1994), among others—are subject to criticism.

One of the reasons why a modern philosopher and scientist can disqualify Baconian epistemology is to reduce his thinking to method. The importance of recognizing the other facets of his thought is because they reveal what science, in its proper epistemological sense, is for Bacon. Without the understanding of the mystical, the spiritual, and the sacrum in Bacon, he can be understood as a mere materialist or realist who saw phenomena as the ultimate reality and believed in the total correspondence of language, ideas, and logic with that reality. This simple interpretation of Bacon's ideas fails when one evaluates what was said in earlier chapters on gnosis, the idea of truth hidden under phenomena, the critique of deductive and even (false) inductive, and critical logic of language in Bacon. To conclude succinctly, one could say that Baconian thought is more complex and less simplistic than some have supposed.

---

[227] See WHEELER, Harvey. *The Semiosis of Francis Bacon's Scientific Empiricism.* England: Semiotics 133, 2001, pp. 45-47.

4.3 What is Baconian Epistemology? Some Possibilities

Was the Baconian conception of science instrumentalist, falsifiable, objectivist, epistemologically anarchist, historicist, or nonrepresentative realist? Indeed, can the English philosopher (prior to the solidification of modern science) fit into one of these categories? The answer is that taking care that one does not create an anachronism, an approximation can be made if sufficient converging elements exist.[228] But first, these different interpretations of science will be presented briefly. The instrumentalist model believes that science should not be considered for the ability to provide man with knowledge of things, but for future events.

For its proponents, science's description of phenomena does not necessarily correspond to reality. Observable entities can be described correctly, but pure, unobservable, and only theoretical sciences are liable to have considerable failures – which incapacitate the scientist's factuality of his thesis. Hence, the theories as "instruments" that foresee future actions of entities, ensuring the coherence of scientific work. The fallibilist position has already been defined in the previous section. A. F. Chalmers (1939-) considered the position of Lakatos (1922-1994) objectivist, using this term to designate the Lakatosian features of rejecting the hasty and not (methodologically) reasoned elaboration of theses, relating heuristics, scientific methodology, research programs, its "protective belt", "firm core", "progressive programs", "recessive programs", "refutability", among other concepts, in order to provide the scientist with the objectivity of his research and his conclusions. Paul Feyerabend (1924-1994) developed the idea that science does not obey specific methods and that the scientist can resort to unconventional methods to defend his thesis, since there is no absolute criterion to define what is true or which science model is correct – according to Feyerabend, nor does modern science rigidly follow a single model. He called this epistemological anarchism. The historicist model was studied by Thomas Kuhn. He came to the conclusion that scientists are not only logical or rational but also people within and influenced

---

[228] See BACON, Francis. *The Advancement of Learning* [1605], p. 145.

by a historical-social context. The advent of the scientific revolution, according to Kuhn, would be the substitution of a paradigm of thought by another in the scientific world – in a process that goes from normal science, through crisis, to extraordinary science and revolution. This paradigm emerges not only from rational, logical, or objective factors but also from historical-social issues inherent in human subjectivity. Yet the nonrepresentative realistic model advocated by A. F. Chalmers argues that scientific theories should not be considered as corresponding to the facts of nature but rather, by accepting the realistic language of the common observer, they should have a greater applicability than that delimited by proponents of instrumentalism, broadening the understanding that the latter have of the new forecasts and being more open to possibilities of greater speculation about theoretical entities.[229]

Bacon, because he is not a modern scientist and because he is a complex thinker, cannot be satisfactorily categorized as a proponent of one or more of these theories. Nevertheless, there are similarities between him and some of the others. In the first place, Bacon was realistic and methodological. This brings him closer to Popper's falsifiable model and Lakatos' objectivism. Secondly, he believed in a truth that could be obtained at the end of the whole inductive

---

[229] Ellis calls the new essentialism a modern tendency to dialogue with the old conception that the thinkers had with nature and to resize the idea of metaphysics, situating it with modern science. He says, "The new essentialism that is now being developed as a metaphysics for modern science is compatible with this intuition. It is not a reversion to Aristotelianism, or an attempt to resurrect medieval visions of the nature of reality. On the contrary, its origins are decidedly in century XX. Essentialist distinctions among natural types of substances, for example, depend on the existence of quantum discretion in the world, for it is this discretion at the quantum level that ultimately guarantees that such distinctions are real and ontologically based – not just distinctions we have taxation on nature for our own purposes [...] Q. 5 The new essentialism is a modern version of this ancient theory. New essentialists, like the ancients, insist that the same things, constituted in the same way, from the same basic components, would have to behave in the same way in any other world in which they may exist, for what they do or the what they could do is of their essence. The things that exist are therefore to determine what the laws of nature are, rather than the laws determining how things should behave. But the new essentialism, unlike the old, is a metaphysical for a modern scientific understanding of the world." ELLIS, Brian. *The Philosophy of Nature: The Guide to the New Essentialism*. Chesham: Acumen, 2002, p. 1.

process – hidden from the method embodied in parts and seems to limit the phenomena observable by the scientist. This notion can bring it closer to instrumentalism and the nonrepresentative realist model. Thirdly, Bacon rejects anarchist and historicist positions, due to both limiting the methodology. Thus, from the science-related theses discussed above, Bacon is closer to Popper's realism (fallibilism), instrumentalism, and the non-representative realism of A. F. Chalmers.[230] However, there are important differences between Bacon and these three models. Bacon is not (1) a falsifier in Popper's sense that the scientist can never think of irrefutable or non-falsifiable scientific truths; (2) he is not an instrumentalist in the sense that the proponents of this school understand, due to openly advocating the instrumental use of non-observable entities and making predictions 3) and is also not a nonrepresentative realist in the Chalmers sense, because phenomenon, although it is real to the observer's eye this observation cannot be overlooked, and must be expressed by the scientist as not corresponding to the things themselves. The similarities and dissimilarities between Bacon and some of the theses presented on science reveal that,

1. It is necessary to discard the thesis that Bacon is a naive realist incapable of conceiving that observable phenomena do not delimit the totality of the real,

2. Because the complexity that unites two paradoxes, that of realism and that of the mystical idea of absolute unobservable truth to be factually found at the end of induction, precludes a simplistic thesis about Bacon's epistemology,

3. Adding to this the fact that the whole of Bacon's philosophy transcends the inductive method and that misinterpretations about the author emerge from the inability to conceive this, reducing it to the induction theory.

Without wishing to put an end to the subject, but aiming to broaden the discussion of Bacon's epistemology[231] in the academic world

---

[230] CHALMERS, A. F. *What is Science, Anyway?* Trad. br. Raul Fiker. São Paulo: Editora Brasiliense, 1993, p. 195.

[231] See BACON, Francis. *The Advancement of Learning* [1605], pp. 130-150.

by providing guidelines, the research presented in this section concludes, raises another important point in the next section.

4.4 A Techné

In his book *Francis Bacon and the Foundation of Science as Technology*, Oliveira relates Bacon's science to technique, arguing that in Bacon technological advancement is a consequence of the advance of science – in the sense that Greek philosophy on mechanical art, is not taken as a rhetorical device, as the Sophists did. He states:

> [In Bacon] maker's knowledge is a notion that associates knowledge with creation. Briefly, it suggests that we know something when we do and that when we do something it is because we know [...] the connection between knowledge and construction shows a remarkable change in the traditional opposition between *epistémé* and *techné* [...] This change is, in a way, the axis of that which is called the substitution of the "why" for the "how."[232]

As a supporter of the meticulous observation of the method,[233] it is clear that Bacon gives the theory a status inferior to the status attributed to the use of artifacts from the techné for the attainment of knowledge. Techné, by its very nature, requires method, system, artifice, and applicability. The method for the English philosopher was not to serve as a speculation for future generations of scientists, but as a practical legacy for the scientists of his time to facilitate future work, so that the use of the learned technique could replace the necessity of the theoretical and speculative resources that seek to unveil the foundation of the method or what theoretically determines it. For example, in the present day, when an electrical engineer studies the distribution of electricity in a city to be built, he

---

[232] OLIVEIRA, Bernardo Jefferson de. *Francis Bacon and the Foundation of Science as Technology*. Belo Horizonte: UFMG, 2002, p. 141.
[233] See BACON, Francis. *Novum Organum*, p. 59.

does not need to understand all the theoretical details of Faraday's (1761-1867) experiment on electricity and magnetism, this it is not necessary to have a total understanding of the theories, objections, and uncertainties that involve the phenomenon, but only the theses that are reasonable and accepted, and especially the thing itself: electric energy in full operation. The distribution of the electric energy already presented by the technique does not require an exhaustive theorization on how the theoretician first managed to intervene in natural phenomena and make them useful to men. Faraday's Law of Induction, Gauss's Law, Maxwell's Equations, and Ampère-Maxwell's Law were added to the first event that gave rise to an extraordinary change in the world: electrical power. Every student of electromagnetic phenomena, the ripples, electric fluxes from laws, predecessor equations, no longer has to start from scratch, speculating about everything. Broadening the example, the student of robotics, computer science, medical examinations, laser surgeries, creators of televisions, mobiles, and airplanes do not need to speculatively discuss every detail of an earlier tradition or even begin the scientific school again, returning to pure theory to see if the whole technological tradition is right or wrong. Even the so-called electricity generators, such as hydroelectric plants and nuclear power plants, depend on these theoretical complexities of their predecessors to exist. Similarly, mathematical formulas are also used in physics, without knowing the theory synthesized in the formulas.

Some may counter-argue: The accuracy of the facts in which the method, put into practice, demonstrates its functionality, and makes doubt unnecessary. This exactness in science is accurate and, by definition, eliminates questioning. Responding to this counterargument, it must be said that the idea of exact science applied in empirical science is not intended to eliminate any possibility of error in this science but to reduce that possibility. The functionality or applicability of a theory cannot reduce the possibility of error to zero. Moreover, it would reduce empiricism to mathematics, eliminate the differences between theory and practice, transform scientific truth into eternal truth, deny any concept of falsification, and contradict the very concept of induction and scientific method. Therefore, one must conclude that techné , if not counterbalanced by *theoria* or speculation, reduces the world to mechanism and impairs the development of rationality.[234]

Bacon wanted to advance the technique. However, he also wanted the advance of knowledge. Without studying the influence of the mystical on him, one can hastily come to the conclusion that Bacon was a mere mechanist and that he was concerned only with the practical accuracy of formulas synthesized in scientific method, not taking into account the theory behind the formulas. Mechanical-technical pragmatism would be a definition for him.

Bacon wanted the technique to reach a truth created before using the technique. The technique, however, has a primordial importance, for it surpasses the theory after the application of the inductive method and serves the theory in two moments: the moment before the method and the final moment, and the point of arrival of the method, which is the knowledge absolute. The knowledge acquired by the technique is superior, while the technique fulfills its purpose. Prior knowledge of technique and post-technical knowledge, if understood in the teleological background, however, make the technique, in one instance, a servant of truth to be revealed in nature. Bacon thus contributes to the existence of technological society, but the interpretation of Bacon's philosophy does not take into account the idea that if technique follows a purpose for it determined and created before it is tested, it will fall into the error of confusing technology with a pragmatic and mechanical technicality that reduces theoretical elements to zero on its path to the discovery of truth.

---

[234] Rossi demonstrates, for example, that in the medieval world an unverifiable element in nature as the art of memory was important in assisting empiria. He says, "The harsh polemic against the magicians of memory does not hinder the techniques of memorization as such, but attempts to reduce them at the level of occult and magical arts. When applied to the most serious purposes of rhetoric, and embedded in the logic of persuasion, memory still has a function in the new encyclopedia of science. The Baconian project of a *scientia universalis, mater reliquarum scientiarum* presents itself as it had in the Lullian tradition, its justification and its foundation in the unity of the world." ROSSI, Paolo. *The Universal Key: Arts of Memorization and Combinatorial Logic from Lulio to Leibniz*. Trad. br. Antonio Angonese. Bauru: EDUSC, 2004, p. 224.

4.5 Induction and Ethics

The scientist, for Bacon, is naturally ethical. To strive for excellence, he practices ethics to undertake his work as a scientist.[235] Indeed, this is possible because, in Bacon, the end of science is social progress. Induction and social harmony are, in this conception, deeply related, and it may even be said that induction is the cause and effect of social harmony. Scientists present themselves as the ambassadors of ethics, since they must lead the world towards both progress and harmony. Rovighi maintains that duty in Bacon refers to professional duties, which are defined by men of science.[236] Taylor argues that benevolence in Bacon, overcoming suffering, and the welfare of the social aspect are the central intents for the cognition of reality, and knowledge is the domain over reality.[237] Consequently, "progress" and "new" are ideas which, for Bacon, not only describe laboratory achievements in science, but also the overcoming of social problems, which are related to false knowledge. True inductive knowledge is not a knowledge that brings benefits only to laboratory technicians, but also changes in all spheres of social life, whether in the economy, in the arts, or in the problem of violence and war, among other examples. Thus Bacon, not repeating exactly the ethics of the virtues of Plato and Aristotle, and not anticipating Kant's deontological ethics, seems to give science the power to legislate about morality, as if scientific discoveries reveal facts that should be obeyed and thus, self-imposed truth, as law. However, the mystical and theological elements that influence the teleology that Bacon gave to his science must be respected. For example, Bacon's appreciation of the idea of absolute knowledge, which has Gnostic roots, is his idea of the hidden truth in nature and his respect for the Protestant religion, reflected in his scientific language – idol theory,

---

[235] See OLIVEIRA, Bernardo Jefferson de. *Francis Bacon and the Foundation of Science as Technology*. Belo Horizonte: UFMG, 2002, pp. 204-205, 209.

[236] See SONIA, Vanni Rovighi. *History of Modern Philosophy - From the Scientific Revolution to Hegel*. Trad. Marcos Bagno and Silvana Cobucci Leite. São Paulo: Loyola, 1999, p. 32.

[237] See TAYLOR, Charles. *Sources of the Self: The Making of the Modern Identity*. Cambridge: Cambridge University Press, 1998, pp. 84-85.

the idea of overcoming errors, etc. – provides strong evidence that Bacon had the preconceived notion that science would never destroy mystical elements of life. He said that science should not interfere with religion-apt to individual delight, according to Fiker's observation.[238] In this way, the Baconian ethics is not reduced to the method, although it depends on it. Rather, inductive method is the cause of ethics in Bacon, but the concept of inductive method is contradictory in the English philosopher so that Baconian induction could not be what it is without the complex influences of a mystique that transcends method.

The panlogism and the possibility of describing all reality in a mathematical formula were Bacon's desires. This exhaustive knowledge[239] of reality puts an end to "evil," that is, for Bacon, polylogism will give men dominion over the real, so that, overcoming the epistemic problems between subject and object, and there being now total verisimilitude between the two – or better, total correspondence between them (subject and object), knowledge is equivalent to the realization of the will. The effort to knowing (ratio) is, in this case, credible to the satisfaction of willing (*voluntas*). Therefore, there is no longer any "evil" or anything that comes from the lack of knowledge and the dissatisfaction of the will. The maxim 'to know is power"[240] can be extended to "knowledge of everything equals power for everything." Thus, the overcoming of original sin and the conquest of the dominion of nature—as studied in the second chapter—lead to peace, social harmony, and ethics.

---

[238] See FIKER, Raul. *The Knowing and Knowing in Francis Bacon*. São Paulo: New Alexandria, 1996, pp. 208-213.

[239] BACON, Francis. *Novum Organum* [1620], pp. 15, 21.

[240] It resembles the Aristotelian metaphor of induction as a battlefield. See GROARKE, Louis. *An Aristotelian Account of Induction: Creating Something from Nothing*, p. 296.

4.6 Scientific Neutrality

The theory of idols is a critique of the lack of neutrality in empirical work,[241] as well as a critique of the theoretical and linguistic prejudices of men. However, Bacon was once again paradoxical. Despite formally defending neutrality, in practice, he was not neutral. Beforehand, he had a great preconceived project for his science. *Instauratio magna* had never gone through the inductive process, but the idea of order and instituting this project are assumed to be factual and guide Baconian rhetoric as to the importance of the inductive method. He has never "started from scratch" in his scientific work. It is true that he was a sophisticated, scholarly thinker, and that his criticism was correct in several respects, but the spirit of his time, still not dominated by the laic and "disenchanted" spirit of modernity, made him take for granted natural ideas that are not in contemporary times. In other words, the perenniality of religion and mysticism are not facts that are evident to modern man, contrary to what was thought in Bacon's time.

By limiting "prejudices" to the minimum, Bacon might think that ideas that are classified as mystical belonged to the category of "natural," representative of things of nature, and were not preconceptions. For example, Bacon believed that physiognomy, discredited by modern science as superstition, was a scientific activity and therefore not to be confused with non-scientific preconceptions. In fact, Bacon's "naturalness" and "neutrality" can only be understood by the mentality of someone who has not yet been (critically) superstitious of the post-Newtonian world, a world in which spirit and nature are separated in such a way that the scientist does not have the possibility to classify instances as "natural", "factual" or "scientific" – a concept that puts the autonomy of nature, understood as a mechanism with its laws reducible to matter. Although not yet a modern scientist in the full sense of the term, his criticism of both contemporary thinkers and of the ancients, and his defense for overcoming the prejudices of those

---

[241] See BACON, Francis. *Novum Organum* [1620], p. 149.

who preceded him, required that he be more coherent in practice with his theory, and avoiding being an advocate of neutrality while he was not neutral. While not "naive," he had his limitations.

4.7 *The Royal Society, Science, and Politics*

Bacon had great ambitions for the Royal Society. He wanted this society to be sponsored by the sovereign of his country.[242] If the state recognized the central value of a well-organized scientific society for the country and invested in it financially, the whole country would win. This is Bacon's conception. With the ongoing scientific project, all areas of social life would be positively affected. The harmony of knowledge begins with a well-designed scientific project. Poetry, painting, music, law, literature, among other areas, would be—directly or indirectly—influenced by the objective truth that science would bring to the world and which would define the very concept of reality for the cosmos. Just as beliefs considered scientific in the past had been reduced to superstitions in Bacon's time because of science—like the reality of the existence of certain monsters—he reasoned that if changing a certain epistemological paradigm was possible with the discovery of a portion of reality by science, when the true inductive method was applied, and the full knowledge of reality was reached, then the whole of life and society would be affected. Therefore, science is the ambassador of a new world, a better society, and a better world.

The Royal Society should, therefore, fulfill the mission of bringing truth to the world and leading it, starting in England, to a new stage in its history, which could be classified as the end of history or, at least, the conventional idea of "history."

The Royal Society did not become what Bacon had dreamed of, despite the enormous prestige it received. His project was far too ambitious. Even so, Bacon's legacy to the Royal Society is undeniable. Thomas Sprat says (1635-1713): "I will appoint only one great man, one who can imagine the whole of this enterprise as it is now instituted:

---

[242] See BACON, Francis. *The Advancement of Learning* [1605], p. 145.

the great Lord Bacon."[243] Its legacy reaches beyond the Royal Society and extends to the scientific academies in general. Christiaan Huygens (1629-1695), speaking of the *Académie des Sciences de Paris*, says: "The main occupation of this Assembly, and the most useful one, should, in my opinion, be to work, in natural history, more or less on Bacon's purpose."[244] There is, therefore, no denying that, despite its limitations and inconsistencies, Bacon cannot be denied a chair of honor in the world of scientific academies, nor in the Royal Society in England.

Bacon was not only a man who dealt theoretically with politics but a man who experienced politics in practice. He held a variety of important public positions in the English society of his day, from youth to the last stage of his life. In 1584, when about twenty-three years old, he was elected to the House of Commons. Later, during the reign of the monarch Jaime I, he served as attorney general (1607), general prosecutor (1613), guard of the seal (1617), and chancellor (1618). He also received the titles of Baron of Verulam and Viscount of St. Albano. He was then charged with corruption in 1621, five years before his death, and was prohibited from holding public office – in addition to a fine, which should not overshadow its previous political legacy.

He had personal contact with another influential philosopher of his time, Thomas Hobbes (1588-1679), and influenced Puritans who held important positions in parliament. He was also believed to have been a propagandist of Rosicrucianism, whose aim was to restructure the philosophical, scientific, political in England and the rest of the world.

In the book *Essays on Morals and Politics*, Bacon makes several considerations about the social problems that surrounded him. Issues such as financial prosperity, war, economic-political-cultural expansionism, religiosity in the public sphere, among others, are important to him. The scientific progress advocated by Bacon could

---

[243] SPRAT Apud JAPIASSU, Hilton. *Francis Bacon: The Prophet of Modern Science*, p. 65.

[244] HUYGENS Apud JAPIASSU, Hilton. *Francis Bacon: The Prophet of Modern Science*, p. 65.

bring positive consequences to the maritime-commercial expansion during this period of discovery of the new world and cultural expansionism. Although no attempt is made here to state the extent of his influence, it is no exaggeration to say that Bacon's ideas were useful to British commerce – the title of Queen of the Seas was given to England for the British East India Company, for the territorial expansion of the kingdom, and English economic growth. Bacon provides some practical advice aimed at improving the state:

> The first remedy or preventive measure is to eliminate, by all means possible, that material cause to which we allude, that is, deprivation and poverty in the State. The means to do this include opening up all trade routes, harmonizing and reorganizing them, giving new impetus to industry, eliminating idleness altogether, suppressing waste and excesses through sumptuary laws, creating new incentives for agriculture, to regulate commercial prices and to moderate taxes and taxes, etc.[245]

Since his conception of science was inseparable from the practical political-social sphere,[246] Bacon's panlogism or gnosis of science would impact everything from minor and domestic issues to larger issues and the universalization of ideas. Topics such as economics, foreign policy, law, geopolitics, as well as the theme of violence and war, would derive from induction, the source of all knowledge. Politics and natural philosophy relate to this because it is in the realm of nature that the philosopher-scientist is able to act politically in favor of society and social harmony. Hence the need for the politician to be wise, to know, to study, and to be improved through the study of natural philosophy. There is no room for a proto-communist political ideal in Bacon. Indeed, the need for a scientific elite in the rulership of the nation makes it seem like an aristocratic one that would hardly accept liberal democracy, despite the existence of ideas that favor the practice of the free market, commercial expansion, and the defense of the private property. He was in favor of the monarchy

---

[245] BACON, Francis. *Essays on Morals and Politics*. Trad. br. Edson Bini. Bauru-SP, EDIPRO, 2001, p. 5.
[246] BACON, Francis. *Novum Organum* [1620], p. 59.

and wrote the *Advancement of Learning* to the English monarch James I. For him, there should be cooperation between the monarch and the noble scientists of the Royal Society so that both were the dignitaries of a new time of progress. He believed it was easier to advance his intent to monarchy. In addition, his public position and the positions that he received made him more eager to have his suit heard by the sovereign. In fact, Bacon militated politically for his cause, the cause of induction, science, and progress. He believed in it and fought politically for it.

4.8 Bacon, General Systems Theory, and Epistemology of Systems Thinking

Menna and Wheeler agree on Bacon's influence on C. S. Peirce (1839-1914). There is no objection to the thesis that there was a certain influence of Bacon on the American philosopher. However, this work does not see support for Menna's thesis that Bacon proposed, like Peirce, an abduction, not an induction, as his method, associating the English philosopher with modern pragmatism.[247] Certainly, some ideas existing in the present world can trace their origin to a certain interpretation of Bacon. Wheeler sees in the English philosopher not only an influence on Peirce's semiosis, but also an influence on the triadic system consisting of phenomena, noumenon, and schematism, by Kant (1724-1804).[248] However, neither Peirce nor Kant attempted to construct an *Instauratio Magna*, in the mold of Lord Verulam. This raises a new question, however: Is there any contemporaneous school of thought that resembles Bacon's total project?

The General Systems Theory (GST) and Epistemology of Systems Thinking (ST) seem to present themselves, like Bacon, as not properly modern or properly postmodern ways of scientific knowledge. Both seem to use what is best in modern rationalism and inductivism, and the best of postmodern holism, similar to the proposal of *Instauratio*

---

[247] See MENNA, Sergio. *Bacon, Peirce and the Intensive Inferences*. Argentina: V Jornada Peirce.

[248] See WHEELER, Harvey. *The Semiosis of Francis Bacon's Scientific Empiricism*. England: Semiotics 133, 2001, pp. 45-47.

Magna and the division of Bacon's knowledge. However, in order to affirm the existence or not of some relation between them and the English philosopher, some warnings and observations become necessary.

In the first place, one has to say once again that one cannot create an anachronism in an academic study. Bacon lived long before these theories, and in a quite different context, so his thinking cannot be confused with such theories, in a reductionist way, simply because of a few similarities. Secondly, it is necessary to reveal what General Systems Theory and Epistemology of Systems Thinking involves. Thirdly, and finally, once the previous stages have been overcome, one should compare them to Bacon by investigating their similarities and differences.

These two schools of thought originate from a historical context different from that of Bacon. Both are post-Newtonian, post-Darwinian, post-Einsteinian, and involve contemporary electricity governing the robotic world and computers, quantum physics, and nuclear chemistry. Bacon, on the contrary, wrote prior to all this, living in an age of unquestioning acceptance of Copernicus' heliocentrism. These schools oppose the technocratic mechanistic model of science, which is reductionist, but they are no longer faced with the enchanted-mystical world in which Bacon lived, before the disenchanted world (Max Weber). The paradigm of mechanism is proper to their context, but not to the context of Bacon. The fact that the spirit-mysticism-enchantment problem is not proper to the scientific method, as such, in either Bacon or these theories, does not prevent it from being said that because of this historical spirit there was a greater dimension of theoretical possibilities for the scientist in the time of Bacon than that which exists in the mechanical world governed by autonomous and already deciphered laws. The mystery of the world in Bacon's time gave the scientist the impression that there should be "something more" beyond the phenomena, something to be unveiled. In the mechanical world, nature no longer appears as mysterious, but like a clock whose mechanism has already been deciphered, repeating its function of cosmic equilibrium by determined laws. If, with Bacon, the scientist ran the risk of being superstitious, the theorists of the General Systems Theory and Epistemology of Systems Thinking face the danger of being too mechanistic and reductionist. Yet another factor is decisive for the impossibility of dealing with the relationship between them and Bacon: Bacon's immediate past involved speculative rather mechanistic science, and its intention was to found a new science that would achieve practical results for society, while the immediate past of the current critics of the experimental method is a scarcely speculative and strongly mechanistic science, the intention of which is not to deny the positive practical results already established, but to reform this same science by maintaining its postulates and its history.

The General Systems Theory[249] was developed by the Austrian biologist Ludwig von Bertalanffy (1901-1972). This theory has important assumptions that are opposed to the purely mechanistic and reductionist idea of science. It believes that there is a tendency for convergence between the natural and social sciences, a tendency or integration that is capable of grounding a general theory of systems, that is, a theory that unifies fields or sectors of research, whether empirical or non-empirical. All sciences are seen as interdependent. Some of the fundamental concepts of GST are:

1. Entropy, according to which every system deteriorates,
2. Syntropy or negative entropy, according to which forces contrary to entropy are developed so that the system does not die,
3. Fitness for balance (called homeostasis),
4. Heterostasis, according to which for each failure in the system there is a tendency to equilibrium.

If classical mechanics is seen as "closed" in itself, GST proposes to be "open" to interactions with the environment. The closed systems would be those that do not interact with the environment in which they are inserted, being the isolated systems constant in their entropy. The important concept of synergy, in turn, is that

---

[249] See BERTALANFFY, Ludwig. *General System Theory: Foundations, Development, Applications*. George Brazilier, New York, 2013.

of interaction between the elements that make up a thing, an interaction that structures and orders it. This cyclic process in which there is entropy forces contrary to entropy, and self-regulation, is also called feedback. Thus, by not individualizing a field of study or a studied entity, the General Systems Theory seeks to study the complete system, treating the parts as integral to the whole.

The theory of Epistemology of Systems Thinking,[250] in turn, opposes what is believed to be the mechanical-reductionist model of science and defend interdisciplinarity between the sciences, whether empirical or non-empirical. It is so closely related to GST that it is difficult to differentiate between them. The latter, however, because of the work during the 1950s and 1960s of Bertalanffy,[251] a biologist, has a more biological historical background, having influenced the study of Systemic Biology. The ST, in turn, has as some of its most important postulates:

- A system is composed of parts;
- All these parts relate to each other, either directly or indirectly;
- The views, whether of an observer or of several observers, give a "limit" to the system;
- Two systems can interconnect – one can house the other;
- The system occurs within space-time.

The ST contrasts the paradigms of mechanistic science with its paradigms.

- The presupposition of simplicity is opposed to the presupposition of complexity.
- Under the assumption of stability, it is opposed by the assumption of instability

---

[250] Ver CULL, Jane. *Living Systems: An Introductory Guide to the Theories of Humberto Maturana & Francisco Varela*. Australia: Midland Typesettles, 2013.

[251] Hammond states that Bertalanffy's work can be compared to Francis Bacon. See HAMMOND, Deborah. *The Science of Synthesis: Exploring the Social Implications of General Systems Theory*. University Press Colorado, Colorado, 2010.

- The presupposition of objectivity contrasts with the presupposition of intersubjectivity.

The idea of simplicity is flawed, according to the ST, because, considering the microscopic entity as simple, it establishes itself in the study of this entity separating it from the whole, which prevents real knowledge. The idea of stability fails to reduce the phenomenon to a stable entity that can be studied mechanically, including under the strictness of supposed natural laws and without exceptions. The idea of objectivity fails to believe the world as the eye sees it. It thinks of nature as a simple, knowable entity to be studied by a subject who is separated from it. This makes it difficult to understand the complexity of both nature and the self as part of the natural world. For ST, nature, being complex, does not give the researcher the right to study an entity separately. Rather, one must study everything as part of a whole, and also investigating the whole in part. Since nature is unstable, it must be seen as a multiplicity of phenomena that should not be studied in isolation. Intersubjectivity must thus replace the idea of objectivity because phenomena are not separate from the observer. Phenomena and observers are intertwined. The ST understands that not only phenomena and observers, but each observer is connected to others also.

What are the similarities and dissimilarities between GST, ST, and Bacon? First, the similarities between them will be listed here. Both GST, ST, and Bacon believe that:

1. All sciences are interconnected;
2. That empirical science is linked to social issues;
3. That empirical science should not fall into the error of reducing reality to its field of study;
4. That empirical knowledge has implications on the knowledge of the whole, even on non-empirical parts.
5. That reductionism must be rejected in favor of a more holistic view of science.

Despite all the similarities above, there are serious dissimilarities between GST, ST, and Bacon's thinking. These differences make it impossible to classify GST and ST as "Baconians,"[252] or state that Bacon was a mere precursor of GST and ST. Among the main dissimilarities are the following:

1. Proponents of the ST, such as Humberto Maturama (1928) and Francisco Varela (1946-2001) — proponents of the autopoiesis thesis,[253] according to which living beings are able to self-produce—as well as GST, with its relation with the theory of the evolution of species through the work of Bertalanffy, developed more materialistic ideas than the ideas contained in the whole of Bacon's thought.

2. Both the ST and the GST depart from scientific postulates of modern science, while Bacon is not yet modern scientifically.

3. The practical consequences of the ST and the GST are less favorable to mysticism and religiosity than Bacon wished with his inductive method.

4. The function of the scientist in society has its own teleology that is not in GST and in ST. Even in regard to the similarities between the English philosopher, GST, and ST cannot be used to deny the uniqueness of Bacon and, above all, to his status as a precursor. Rather, it is necessary to recognize the distinctive character[254] of complexity in Bacon's thought, refusing to confuse it, not only with certain postulates and paradigms of modern science but also with certain postulates and essential paradigms of the GST and the ST.

---

[252] See BACON, Francis. *Novum Organum*, I, p.63 apud ROSSI, Paolo. *Shipwrecks Without Spectators: The Idea of Progress*.

[253] See MATURAMA, Humberto; VARELA, Francisco. *The Tree of Knowledge: The Biological Roots of Human Understanding*. Shambala Publications, Mass, 1992.

[254] Bacon's ideas are stimulating even for a new influx into the study of language. Botvina notes that Bacon's natural philosophy is a universal language. She asserts that the idea of the Adamic language is seen by Bacon as the language of science, for just as Adam in the Garden of Eden spoke pure language, language wholly corresponding to things, science in Bacon has the function of purifying language and "reconnecting" speech to things.

4.9 Summary of Sections 1-8

All sections hitherto, despite the thematic variation, have had a purpose: to investigate Bacon's logical-inductive science. Sections one and eleven stated that:

1. Bacon's inductive science cannot be studied superficially;
2. Ethics, according to Bacon, may be influenced by induction, but not reduced to it;
3. Bacon was not at all a neutral scientist;
4. Bacon was important to the Royal Society for science in general since the end of the Middle Ages; the scientist, for Bacon, is a political being par excellence;
5. There are similarities, but also important dissimilarities between the General Systems Theory, Epistemology of Systems Thinking, and Bacon.

This set of subjects, related to inductive science, allows one to have a precise view of what Bacon understood and, as a consequence of this, also nature. But an issue remains unexplored: is what Bacon understands to be nature or natural phenomena the same as what the ancients understood? This question will be answered in the next section.

The analogy between the Edenic world and Botvina's world of science is to describe the Baconian idea that although common language is full of misunderstandings and not a corresponding reality, the creation of a pure language could achieve this perfect relationship between the thing and the talk about the thing, performing a "translation of the order of the world into language." Dunca compares Bacon's sentence "Religion is the greatest bond of humanity" with the idea of the Analytic Philosophy of Religion that religious experiences are analytic and that religions should be studied not only empirically, but also logically and analytically. For Dunca, Bacon's postulate is an axiom on which the Analytical Philosophy of Religion stands. Pribble alludes to the condemnation that Bacon issues to poetry – notwithstanding the existence of the thesis that he would have been the true writer of Shakespeare's works (1564-1616). For Bacon the poetic language is an imitation of reality and not its description, forming fantasies and producing images that are reduced to rhetoric. Pribble highlights the fact that the rhetoric of the scientist, according to Bacon, must reject the ambiguity—which is present, for example, in

4.10 The Real Causes of Bacon's Critique of the Ancients and Aristotle

There are many treatises by Bacon that can provide an overview of his thinking: *Novum Organum, The Advancement of Learning, The Wisdom of the Ancients, Valerius Terminus, Theory of Heaven,* and *The Intellectual Description of the Globe*. None, however, clearly reveals it. That is why we have so far sought to examine Bacon's ideas, looking at their complexity and paradoxes. For this reason, it must be stated that no ready-made formulas regarding the author have been reached, but there is strong evidence for a rediscovery of Bacon. Rediscovery is now being advanced by new researchers, who have continued to ask: "To what extent was Bacon a forerunner of a new science and to what extent was this a continuation of an ancient scientific tradition?"

---

poetry—and be clear in what it proposes to convey. The example of hieroglyphs is used to show that Bacon recognized that images can convey knowledge. Even without modern alphabets, hieroglyphs succeeded in transmitting knowledge. The letters of the modern alphabet, which were the modern grammar, in turn, should have this same purpose. The semantic content of the prayers coming from the modern alphabet must be to convey a truth not reduced to letters but also transmitted in other ways. The error of ambiguity, of using rhetoric to fantasize things and giving words a value contrary to the value that science gives it, which is to describe the world, can be categorized as a mistake coming from the idols of the theater. In him, the imaginary takes the place of the real, beside the authority of the speaking taking the place of the thing for which the speech points. However, Bacon used non-literalist language for the transmission of knowledge. Even body language was the subject of Bacon's study. In *New Atlantis*, a fable is used for this purpose. The aphorisms were too important to him. What Bacon wants is not to ban poetry, but to prevent ambiguous rhetoric from taking the place of the scientist's descriptive language. McLuhan, studying the theory of communication in Bacon, states that the idea of Cratylus—of Plato's work—that the names of things are linked to things themselves has influenced the emphasis on the study of grammar in medieval philosophy, including influence on mystics, like the alchemists, despite the influence of the non-grammatical method of studying language in Aristotle. Bacon, according to McLuhan, had also been influenced by Cratylus, but his system completely rejected dialectics to Aristotelian rhetoric. For him, Bacon's rhetoric about idols is similar to that of Roger Bacon, who preceded him, and agrees with the belief that human language was affected by the original fall.

It is not difficult to recall some facts about Bacon's relations to the ancients: he referred to the stars as flames, defined circles as "perfect"—although he did not endorse some author's use of the notion of perfect circles—and demonstrated knowledge of the pyramidal form of fire. He also believed in the divine, like most of the ancients. He still did not perceive the problem of language in describing phenomena. Bacon's treatment of the vacuum issue was also praiseworthy. It was superior to that of Aristotle. But the biggest problem to be faced, so to speak, was not this question, not even the idea of atomism, but that of infinity, which seemed to discredit basic ideas about reality in sixteenth-century England, as the created nature of the universe.

Like his predecessors, Bacon was faced with the idea that air, fire, earth, and water were fundamental elements for life. These facts are sometimes not perceived by reductionists regarding the interpretation of Bacon. From all the questions raised throughout this book, we have come to the conclusion that the real causes of Bacon's criticism of the ancients—and especially of Aristotle—

In rhetoric, McLuhan goes on, Bacon uses two modes of aphorism: the esoteric, and therefore proper to the true scientists, and the exoteric, common to the vulgar. The aphorism would be a means by which Bacon would convey knowledge. The observations and creations of axioms would need these aphorisms, which would be useful to the inductive method itself. Finally, McLuhan argues that, since Trivium, Quadrivium, and the study of grammar are important in the pre-modern world, knowledge of etymologies became rather excellent. Studying the etymology of words was like studying their "cause." Thus Bacon's acceptance of the Aristotelian idea of Formal Cause served to seek the "form" of language by etymology and, for alchemists, to investigate the problems of language in order to reconnect them to things because, according to McLuhan, it shows reality, language, and the world, could be in harmony if the scientist mastered language. The book of nature, an encyclopedia, would be unraveled if the scientist knew how to use the right words. For that, he would have to overcome the idolatry that incapacitates the language of achieving its purpose. All these observations and theses on language and the theory of communication in Bacon give this author a greater importance to the study of the foundations of the analytic philosophy of than what has been credited until now.

Well before Frege (1848-1925), Russell (1872-1970), and Wittgenstein (1889-1951), Bacon questioned the theory of the correspondence between language and things, rejected several postulates of Aristotelian logic—among which are the postulates of Aristotle 's own inductive logic, as was seen before—he conceived were not the discoveries of new facts. Bacon was a philosopher who did not completely disengage himself from the ancient world by criticizing the ancient world. He was not a revolutionary in his ideas.[255] Bacon has continued a pre-modern scientific tradition. It was, in fact, groundbreaking and pioneering new ideas about the scientific method, but the idea of an absolute rupture between Bacon and the pre-modern scientific world is wrong. The Baconian induction is still an induction in the general sense, and it is similar to the set of other inductions. His science is still compatible with a "sacred" world. If Bacon was not a medieval man, then he was not a modern man either. The legacy of Bacon for the modern and contemporary world is the subject of the next chapter.

---

language as the conditioner of the transmission of knowledge of the world and undertook a scientific project whose method consisted in observing, testing and describing, through spoken and non-spoken language, reality. See BOTVINA, Renata. *Francis Bacon's Natural Philosophy as Natural Language*. Studies in Logic, Grammar and Rhetoric, 8, 21, 2005, pp. 93-94, 99; PRIBBLE. Paula. *Poetic and Francis Bacon's Ambivalence Toward Language*. St. Cloud State University, Minnesota: Educational Resources Information Center, 1986, p. 28; McLuhan, Eric. *Francis Bacon's Theory of Communication and Media*. McLuhan Studies, Issue 4, Toronto, 1999. DUNCA, Petru. *The Perspective of the Analytic Philosophy of Religion on the Almighty of Gods*. European Journal of Science and Theology, Vol. 8, No. 3, 2012, 27-35.

[255] Take the example given by Lukasiewicz: "Maximilian Wallies, one of the Berlin editors of Aristotle's Greek commentaries, published in 1899 the fragments of Ammonius' commentary on the earlier Analytics and inserted in the preface a scholium of an unknown author found in even a codex in which the fragments of Ammonium were preserved. The scholium is entitled *On All Types of Syllogism* and begins thus: "There are three types of syllogism: the categorical, the hypothetical, and the syllogism (κατὰ πρόσληψιν). From the categorical there are two types: the simple and the compound. Aristotle says that there are only three figures [...] he examines the simple syllogisms, that is to say, which consists of three terms. Galen, however, says [...] that there are four figures, for he examines the composite syllogisms consisting of four figures: he found many of these syllogisms in the dialogues of Plato." The overcoming of Aristotle by Galen is, as it were, a return to Plato: Lukasiewicz, Jan. *Aristotle's Syllogistic: From the Standpoint of the Modern Formal Logic*, Oxford: Oxford University Press, 1951.

5.

BACON AGAINST THE MISINTERPRETATIONS OF HIS LEGACY

THE FINAL CHAPTER IS INTENDED TO UNDERTAKE, IN LIGHT of the studies of the influence of mysticism, religiosity, and considerations on Bacon's inductive method, a critical appraisal of the current interpretations of Bacon's legacy for empirical sciences and contemporary philosophy and, thus, make useful considerations for the re-evaluation of this legacy. In the first section we will talk about Bacon and modernity. In the second section we will investigate Bacon's relationship with the contemporary world. The third section will briefly review the previous sections, concluding with the evaluation of the relevance of this study to the academic field.

5.1 Bacon and Modernity

Modern science, especially after the expansion of the Enlightenment spirit and the so-called "age of reason" (if there was modern science before that), does not accept Hermeticism and religion as sources of scientific inquiry – it is essentially materialistic, anti-spiritualistic, and progressive. It is not that scientists always declare themselves atheists, but that the exercise of science must be distinguished from any form of spiritualism. As the material world is the field of work of the modern scientist, all he needs to know in the role of a scientist is to scrutinize what is before the inductive method.[256] Ideas about anything that avoid the method must be discarded.

"Bacon certainly fought for science to become what it is today,"[257] a hasty researcher might infer. As said in the preceding chapters, the existence of a partial reason for the idea that Bacon is a modern thinker is not denied here. Not everything that has been said about

---

[256] Descartes, contrary to Bacon, sought dialogue with religion academically. In his *Discourse on Method* he argued that the existence of God and the soul were not properly categories of theological faith, but questions of deductive logic, philosophy, rational thought. Distinguishing *res cogitans* from the *res extensa*, Descartes puts the mental and spiritual world, since he admitted that the soul was not reduced to the brain, as a target of academic, philosophical, and scientific scrutiny. "Cartesianism," similar to Baconianism, does not reject the metaphysical sphere of the scope of science. Unlike Baconianism, however, Cartesianism is clearer, more systematic, and seemingly aware of the implications of all its ideas. If Descartes is thought to have contributed to modernity with a system of mechanical thought—it was important for the development of analytic geometry—and for the attempt to remove metaphysical themes from theological and ecclesiastical tutelage, opening space for the weakening of the latter in the academic sphere and for later criticism of this same metaphysics, which would come with thinkers such as Hume and Kant. Bacon sought to safeguard theology and the church (in this case, the Anglican) by putting limits on scientific work. Limits that, if it were contemporary of the later critics of theology, would be sufficient to accuse such people of being unscientific in these acts. See DESCARTES, René. *The Discourse of Method*. Trad. br. Ciro Mioranza. São Paulo: Educational Scale, 2006.

[257] Glanvill (1636-1680), a proponent of the experimental method and famous for his prediction in 1661 that in the future magnetic waves would lead men to communicate with one another on every part of the planet, wrote an essay with the subtitle A Continuation of the New Atlantis, in reference to the *New Atlantis* of Bacon. In it, Glanvill approaches the Baconian academic ideal represented by the House of Solomon to the ideas of the Platonists of Crambridge, among whom were theologians, philosophers, and inductivists such as Benjamin Whichcote (1609-1683) and Nathaniel Culverwel (1619-1651) For Glanvill, Bacon's scientific priests could be exchanged for the young academics of Cambridge Platonism with its metaphysical spectrum, without this being an offense or a direct attack on Baconian ideas. In spite of the Cambridge Platonic criticism of what appeared to be materialism in Bacon, Glanvill was not alone in the connection between his ideas and Bacon. Culverwel, in *The Elegant and Versatile Speech of the Light of Nature*, resorts to Bacon more than once. Whichcote is also considered more critical of Hobbes than of Bacon. See DOROTHEA Krook, *Two Baconians: Robert Boyle and Joseph Glanvill*. Huntington: Huntington Library Quarterly, 1955; CULVERWELL, Nathaniel. *An Elegant and Learned Discourse of the Light of Nature*. Indianapolis: Liberty Fund, 2001.

Bacon is wrong. However, they attempt to show that the partial error in academia about Bacon is significant enough to obstruct the actual understanding of his thinking. The exposition of the English philosopher is not merely an accident of a systematically consistent philosophy or a small lapse of an inextricable interpretation of his larger ideas. Rather, it is a significant part of the whole. Without this, Bacon becomes a caricature,[258] a projection of the modern mind.[259] Bacon was certainly a champion of progress, but his progressivism was not absolute. Baconian rhetoric,[260] which privileged the wholly new, did not factually provide epistemic conditions for starting from scratch. The tension between discourse and practice did not cease in his life. Bacon was not advocating what contemporary conservative

---

[258] Another Baconian was the polymath Samuel Hartlib (1600-1662) who, in addition to an international intelligence agent, created designs for calculation instruments, machines, and engines. As an educator, he attempted to unite the legacy of Bacon and Jan Comenius (1572-1670). He even sought funds for the House of Solomon that Bacon presented in *New Atlantis*. Hezekiah Wooward (1590-1675), a Puritan friend of Hatlib, was also a follower of Bacon and Comenius and sought educational reform in England. Benjamin Worsley (1618-1673), physicist, alchemist and General Surveyor of Ireland, was another Baconian. Gabriel Plattes (1600-1644), who wrote about agriculture, chemistry, geology and metallurgy, was also Baconian. Worsley and Plattes participated in the so-called Hartlib Circle, a name given to a set of correspondences between English and Central European intellectuals. The German "hermetic" theologian Johannes Valentinus Andreae (1586-1654), corresponding with Hartlib, had an interest in creating the Baconian project of absolute knowledge, mathematically synthesized: *pansofia*. Utopian literature had been viewed as an archetype of a reality free from the imperfections of sin and ignorance. In addition to the famous defense of utopia by Thomas More (1478-1535) 169, Andreae and Plattes wrote utopias whose central focus was scientific advancement. In the work *Cristianopolis*, like Bacon, he presents a society founded on science and theology, that is, by a wisdom that knows both nature and the metaphysical mysteries that surround it. Plattes, in the work *Description of the Famous Kingdom of Macaria*, which was also attributed to Hartlib, follows essentially this same direction. See MORE, Thomas. *The Utopia*. Trad. br. Luis de Andrade. São Paulo: Abril Cultural, 1997; ANDREAE, Valentin. *Christianopolis*. New York: Oxford University Press, 1916; To delve into the study of the connection between intellectuals of that time and Bacon See PELTONEN, Markku. *The Cambridge Companion to Bacon*. Cambridge: Cambridge University Press, 2006.

[259] What do all these authors have in common? They were all metaphysical, mystical, or spiritual and directly or indirectly influenced by Bacon.

[260] See BACON, Francis. *Novum Organum* [1620], p. 30-33.

circles call 'archaeofutourism' or 'paleofutourism,' ideas that seek to unite technological progress and the spirit of the new to the essence of the past. If Kuhn's thesis of the paradigm shift caused by scientific revolutions is taken into account, it must be said that the materialist paradigm, while it may be prototypically on the surface of the Baconian method, is not in the complete philosophy of the English author and many of his followers and sympathizers. Why, then, did modern science see itself as an essential break with a past considered obscurantist (seeing mysticism as superstition)? Even if one asserts that Bacon was aware of the anti-metaphysical and materialistic implications of his method,[261] for such an assertion to have academic and non-reductionist content, it must be admitted that it is impracticable to say that all personal beliefs, contradictions, complexity, and the mysticism of Bacon were merely insincere attitudes used as political strategies to impose a new world order. The paradigm shift that came with the impact of these ideas has at least two reasons: (1) the sincere desire to break with the past; and (2) an accident that transcends the original intention and sets up unintended contexts.[262]

---

[261] And also that the materialization of science was a conscious process on the part of the proponents of mechanicism (Descartes, Copernicus, Kepler, and Newton, among others), or that Rosicrucianism and Freemasonry were conscious proponents of a new materialist order of science. To cite an example, the hermeneutic disciple of Heidegger Rudolf Bultmann said that the advances of modern science are concomitant to disbelief in the supernatural world: "One cannot use electric light and radio apparatus, in cases of disease use modern medical and clinical means and, simultaneously, to believe in the world of spirits and miracles." Vico (1668-1744), influenced by Bacon to some extent and well-known proponent of New Science, criticized Descartes' rationalism. David Hume (1711-1776) was wrong when he said: "Bacon's method of reasoning [...] is more pleasing to me when I think it can serve to frustrate dangerous friends or enemies disguised as a Christian religion." BULTMANN, Rudolf. *Believe and Understand*. Trad. br. Altmann, Schlupp and Shneider. São Leopoldo: Sinodal Publishing House, 1987, p. 16; See VICO, Giambattista. *The New Science*. Trad. br. Marco Luchesi. Rio de Janeiro: Record, 1999; HUME, David. *An investigation into Human Understanding*. Trad. br. José de Almeida Marques. São Paulo: UNESP, 1999, p. 171.

[262] It is said that at a meeting in the United States the philosopher Derrida (1930-2004) expounded his thesis on the mismatch between the original intention of the author of a text and the interpretation that the readers give him. At some point in

Like the nascent religions that have interpreted all previous history, as an antecessor for the founding event of their faith filled historical gaps and paradoxes with theses consistent with their theological system, the paradigm of modern science has reinterpreted the history of science and the history of the first modern scientists with preconceptions of modernity, as if aiming to provide modern science with a historical *telos* and a logical development consistent with the idea that modern humans evolved in relation to the pre-modern world. Certainly, Bacon should not be understood within this telos, the evolutionary paradigm, which already existed before Darwin's biological evolutionism (1809-1882). For him, the future was open, the pre-modern world was still real, and the mysteries were still rooted in everyday life. According to Japiassu,

> The whole work of our philosopher [Bacon] is impregnated with references to the biblical texts. In order to substantiate or legitimize his project of 'reform' of human knowledge and understanding, he cannot ignore the introduction, in England, by Henry VIII of the Protestant Reformation. Therefore, it makes extensive use of biblical symbology. He gives the name of Bensalem to his New Atlantis. And the great foundation, which intends to create, denominates 'House of Solomon' or 'College of the Works of the Six Days.' The Aristotelian-medieval philosophy is so vehemently rejected, is because it considers it religiously

---

the meeting someone uses the Derridian thesis to make a critique of religion. The philosopher replies that he did not intend to attack religions. He hears, however, the rejoinder that his intention was not so important, since the text was being interpreted not from the author's intention but on the basis of what the text was for the readers. This example, whether spoken or undocumented, even though it may be untrue, illustrates a real fact: there are limits to the scope of authorship of the consequences of their works. Even if the consequences of their works are to some extent in accordance with the original intention of the author, they can go beyond and follow the paths originally wanted. This is referred to here as an accident that forms a new paradigm of the work. It comes to be seen by a new look, by a review, from a restart and everything is then interpreted according to this new paradigm. The incommensurability of the new that underlies this rupture, this cut, this paradigm shift, is like an epistemological twist that gives new meaning to things and remakes history. See as source of this oral history the video Postmodern Hermeneutics at https://www.youtube.com/watch?v=ygnvtoBrU-k.

ruthless and in opposition to the authentic biblical teachings.²⁶³

Bacon connects knowledge to enlightenment, which in turn imposes on the enlightened the mission of propagating knowledge and rebelling against the blindness of ignorance – note that the symbols of light, enlightenment, and blindness are also present in the biblical texts:

> To say that the blind habit of obedience is safer loyalty than the sense of duty taught and understood is to assert that a blind man may tread more safely guided by a guide than a man is from sight illuminated by a light. And it is beyond discussion that knowledge makes spirits meek, noble, ductile, and docile to government, while ignorance makes them contumacious, refractory, and seditious, and the evidence of time confirms.²⁶⁴

The inductive method, therefore, cannot be contrary to the paradigm of the spirit. Bacon was not an Enlightenment ahead of time.²⁶⁵ If, incidentally, some of his ideas were used by the

---

²⁶³ JAPIASSU, Hilton. *Francis Bacon: The Prophet of Modern Science*. São Paulo: Letras e Letras, 1995, pp. 59-60.

²⁶⁴ BACON, Francis. *The Advancement of Learning* [1605], p. 32.

²⁶⁵ When the French revolutionaries replaced the traditional religion of their country with the worship of the Goddess of Reason and built a new calendar, stripped of the reference to Christ, they were certainly imbibed by the ideal of progress and believed that knowledge and rationality would bring freedom, equality, and fraternity. They may not have foreseen the fate of Robespierre (1758-1794) or Danton (1759-1794), but the events that led to the French Revolution were the consequence of a spirit of rupture with what they believed to be obscurantism. The dialectics of the French revolutionaries' struggle against the absolutism of Louis XIV and of a nascent theoretical justification of the national states under the iron hand of the monarchs should not be denied, but theoretically the enlightenment of the French Revolution was more than a punctual struggle. In it, the idea of the new and the progress was essential. Although men such as Voltaire (1694-1778) defended the Huguenots, and proponents of the revolution were Masons or imbued with some sort of mysticism, the French Enlightenment, compared to Bacon—and ideas and practices of other authors cited in the previous section—was more directed to modern materialism and made a greater rupture with the world that preceded it. The encyclopedism of Diderot (1713-1784) and D'alembert (1717-1783) was not equivalent to the *Novum Organum*,

Enlightenment,[266] they were used for purposes that went beyond Bacon's initial intentions. To fail to notice this is an injustice to the English philosopher and unduly groups him with the French of the eighteenth century.[267]

Among the incompatibilities between Bacon and the Enlightenment are:

1. The rejection of the monarchy and the favoring of the republican spirit, whereas Bacon saw himself as a faithful subject of his king, to whom he dedicated *The Advancement of Learning*;

2. The use of scientific rhetoric to oppose established Christianity, whether Catholic or Protestant, when Bacon

nor Condorcet's *(1743-1794) Essay on the Historical Picture of the Human Spirit*, equivalent to *The Advancement of Learning*.

[266] To make a comparison, even superficially, between some data from the Baconian division of the study of the world and Enlightenment encyclopedism, it follows the simple scheme found in Japiassu: "1. *The memory sciences* are subdivided into: a. history of the generations, relative to the things of the sky, to the meteors, to the volcanic phenomena, to the earth, to the seas. Natural History: b. history of monsters; b1. History of the arts; b2. Ecclesiastical history; Civil history: c. history pure and simple; c1. Literary history, retracing the progress of letters, arts and sciences. 2. *The sciences of reason* are as follows: a. First Philosophy or Science of Axioms; b. Natural sciences (natural sciences and physics); Human sciences (logic, ethics and politics); 3. The sciences of the imagination, aiming at an interpretation, in the sense of the new science, of the set of fables and literary myths." JAPIASSU, Hilton. Francis Bacon: *The Prophet of Modern Science*, pp. 46-47.

[267] For a comparison of some ideas concerning the social impact of his science and the purpose of the Enlightenment, it follows Secco's exposition: "Bacon offers several reasons for the strong investment in research, and for the control of nature. If, on the one hand, all human beings would be benefited by the invention of many works, on the other, governments would have as a return a greater docility on the part of the citizens, since the satisfaction of the necessities, for Bacon, makes the man more susceptible to the acceptance of basic norms of coexistence. In addition to the above-mentioned reasons for hope that serve to convince the whole society of the importance of investing in this new form of knowledge, Bacon tries to establish a science that gives an account of the new panorama that presents itself to the "modern" as an obligation of his time." SECCO, Márcio. *Truth and Method in Francis Bacon*. Master's Dissertation – Pro-Rectory of Research and Post-Graduation, Federal University of Santa Catarina. Florianópolis, 2004, p. 15.

remained Anglican to death and was opposed to the use of science to invalidate issues that were properly theological;

3. The revolutionary and bellicose spirit, when Bacon wished to undertake an intellectual and cultural change in society;

4. The use of philosophical theses—among them the idea of egalitarianism, Rousseau's ideas of contractualism and the Good Savage, and the idea of revolution—that were not based on the methodological rigor of Baconian induction;

5. The legacy as more political than scientific, while Bacon wanted science to be a ground political action.[268]

On progress in Bacon, Galvao says:

For the English philosopher, the study should be directed to the phenomena of nature as the only means of achieving a balance between practice and knowledge. It would be up to his successors to new and productive kind of knowledge the substratum of school education.[269]

---

[268] Are the positivists no closer to Bacon? Comte had criticized certain errors of the French revolutionaries and the positivist thinkers. Fustel de Coulanges (1830-1889) proposed the Religion of Mankind as a counterpoint to traditional religions, and the Theory of the Three States of Comte, in which the third (positive) state, surpassing the second (the metaphysical) and the first (theological), testifies that progress is directly proportional to the abandonment of traditional mysticism and evolution towards positive and humanist science that will bring peace and prosperity to society, are incompatible with Bacon's thinking. The positivists, as well as Darwin (1802-1889), who wrote *The Origin of Species* about 70 years after the French Revolution—and whose evolution theory, despite being biological, has political implications and presuppositions, as has already been said in some scholarly works—were influenced by a spirit of progress different from Bacon's. To some extent, there is a continuity between the idea of progress or evolution in the enlightenment of the French Revolution, Darwinian positivism, and biological-political evolutionism, but this continuity is more peripheral than central, more accidental than essential. Those who are properly modern are not Baconians in the full sense of the term. It is erroneous to declare Bacon the father of some of these scientific theses. See HOFSTADTER, Richard. *Social Darwinism in America Thought*. Boston: Beacon Press, 1992.

[269] GALVÃO, Roberto Carlos Simões. *Francis Bacon: Theory, Method, and Contributions to Education*, p. 39.

But Bacon, unlike the scientists who succeeded him,[270] saw in the scientists a priestly, spiritual mission, imagining science inhabiting a temple, representing both science (wisdom, knowledge) and the spirituality of Solomon. The Baconian technical-scientific laboratory is also[271] liturgical-ritual.[272]

How could Bacon be considered a modern scientist in the full sense of the word if the differences attested above are more than historical and contextual differences?[273] Adorno (1903-1969) and Horkheimer (1895-1973) recklessly cite Bacon as the father of experimental philosophy.[274] Already Galvão is correct when he

---

[270] What reasons led to the term "progress" having different meanings in Bacon and in properly modern thinkers? They are varied and the detailed study of them transcends the purpose of this work. However, it is possible to make some pertinent considerations on the subject, in at least four spheres in which these different ideas of progress appeared, namely, a) political, b) cultural, c) epistemic and as technological spheres. Studying the first, one clearly perceives the political abyss between the end of the Middle Ages and the modern world is already structured. The medieval world, though Christian, had not entirely disassociated itself from the pre-Christian tradition of the ancient world. Despite differences in the classification of the divine, there was still a sense of the presence of the deity among the connected civilizations of the world.

[271] BACON, Francis. *Novum Organum* [1620], pp. 40-50.

[272] There is in modernity a rupture not only with religion, but with a spiritual worldview that rules all the continents of the world. It has not only undertaken a critique of Christianity, but also opposed the past of all mankind. In spite of the theses on mesmerism and animal magnetism, which at the time of the Restoration in France faced growing materialism in science, this growing rejection of a whole world of ideas did not cease. For Bacon, religion should have its political and public influence on human life preserved and be untouched by the scientific community. Only sects or false religions would suffer major impacts.

[273] Cultural differences follow a line drawn on political differences. Culture, understood as the ethnic, religious, and moral phenomenon of a people or a group of peoples associated with each other, is very close to the political sphere. Political action can change a culture and a culture can guide political action. What occurred was the transition between renaissance and modernity—an end to feudalism, an increase in population, growth of the bourgeoisie, openness to the international market, exploration of the New World, and scientific discoveries— which gradually changed Europe.

[274] ADORNO; HORKEIMER. *Dialectic of Enlightenment*. Trad. br. Guido Antônio de Almeida. Zahar, Rio de Janeiro, 2006.

says that the "foundation of modern science is born, for example, with the demystification of reality."²⁷⁵ Between Bacon and modern science, there is considerable asymmetry. This asymmetry, in turn, concerns an entire cosmology.²⁷⁶ The epistemological changes that add a new dimension to the teleology of science in modernity have little to do with Bacon's "priestly" and "divine" mission and are not historical accidents. As such, being able to arrive at "the fundamental principles and axioms" was not work for those who were simply "curious and intrusive,"²⁷⁷ but for initiates.²⁷⁸

It is a fact that the work of the inductive scientist, who continues the legacy of their predecessors, can fail because of the contempt that the adepts of technicality sometimes arouse with theoretical speculation. Now, many think that "if the mathematical, physical, or chemistry works, why understand the theoretical foundations that led to its birth?" By doing so they fail to understand the essential point of contact of the theoretical foundations with the technique utilized and, if this same technique no longer provides the intended

---

²⁷⁵ GALVÃO, Roberto Carlos Simões. *Francis Bacon: Theory, Method and Contributions to Education*. R. Inter. Interdisc. interthesis, v.4, jul./dez. 2007, Florianópolis, pp. 38-39.

²⁷⁶ BACON, Francis. *Novum Organum*, p. 50.

²⁷⁷ Ibid., p. 50.

²⁷⁸ Bacon lived in a period prior to Lavoisier (1743-1794), Priestley (1733-1804), and Scheele (1742-1786) and the "discovery" of oxygen, which helped to disassociate the concept of spirit breathing—*ruach* (רוּחַ) in Hebrew, *pneuma* (πνεῦμα) in Greek, *rúḥ* (روح) in Arabic, *peis* in proto-Indo-European—and classifying the new element as gas, helped to delegate the technique of meditation and techniques of yogis to the status no greater than that of stress-relieving therapy, when it was once a philosophical, spiritual, and scientific practice. He also lived before men such as Döbereiner (1782-1849), Gmelin (1788-1853), Dumas (1800-1884), Meyer (1830-1895), Newlands (1837-1898), Mendeleev (1834-1907), and Moseley 1887-1915) who, together with Lavoisier, helped to create the Periodic Table. Nor did he see the concept of moisture in the air, the nature of human blood, or humors being completely disconnected from spiritual concepts. Nor did he witness the protons "discovered" by Rutherford (1871-1937) in the early twentieth century with the help of Goldstein's (1850-1930) work of the previous century, nor the electrons, whose concept was developed on the fundamental basis of magnetism (1868-1957). Goldstein, Milikan, Rutheford, Shuster (1851-1934), Hittorf (1824-1914), and others were "discovered" in the 19th century.

results, they are unable to provide satisfactory answers. This, of course, is an important factor that explains why modern scientists[279] claiming to follow up Baconian inducibility[280] have departed so far from Bacon's purposes for the scientific academy.

5.2 Bacon and the Contemporary World

Like Bacon, contemporary science, especially quantum mechanics, has considered nature more mystically than modern Science (in the full sense of the word). The recognition by David Bohm (1917-1982) of the similarities between his studies and the work of the Indian Krishnamurti (1895-1986) is clear evidence of this. Quantum mechanics has recognized the indeterminacy and complexity involved in the study of the subatomic world in order to consider ideas involving themes similar to those of ancient monism. Heisenberg correctly asserted that formulations of quantum study in the twentieth century go back to the ideas of pre-Socratic philosophers. In this regard, quantum mechanics is reopening the discussion of concepts that classical mechanics considered obsolete and mystical. For example, speculation about whether or not observation can alter the observed thing, whether or not there is a possibility that a non-causal "relation" between entities, whether or not the scientist is empirical, and to recognize that it is impossible to apply the method without methodologically tested preconceptions,

---

[279] For the study of some of the leading proponents of modern science, see COPERNICUS, Nicolaus. *On the Revolution of Heavenly Spheres*. Trad. Eng. Charles G. Wallis. Chicago: Encyclopaedia Britannica, 1952. GALILEO. *Dialogues Concerning the Two New Sciences*. Trad. Ing. H. Crew and A. de Salvio. Chicago: Encyclopaedia Britannica, 1980; GALEN. *On the Natural Faculties*. Trad. Ing. Arthur J. Brock. Chicago: Encyclopaedia Britannica, 1952; HARVEY, William. *An Anatomical Distinction on the Motion of the Heart and Blood in Animals*. Trad. Ing. Robert Willis. Chicago: Encyclopaedia Britannica, 1980; KEPLER, Johannes. *The Harmony of the World*. Trad. Eng. Charles G. Wallis. Chicago: Encyclopaedia Britannica, 1952. DARWIN, Charles. *On the Origin of the Species*. Chicago: Encyclopaedia Britannica, 1952.

[280] BACON, Francis. *Novum Organum* [1620], pp. 94-95.

among other discussions.[281] All of these[282] certainly assess quantum mechanics and Bacon.

However, Bacon's understanding should not be facilitated by wanting to define it as a precursor of quantum mechanics. There are quite a few components of quantum mechanics that are compatible with what has been said so far about Bacon. There are, however, also components that differentiate Bacon from the proposal of quantum mechanics. In the first place, Bacon was epistemologically

---

[281] Contemporary science, also called quantum mechanics, be considered an example of science that is closer to Bacon's original intentions? If not, did quantum mechanics render Baconian philosophy useless? In order to get to know quantum mechanics, it is necessary to know quantum physics. It studies the subatomic particles. The study of smaller elements than the atom – fermions, quarks, bosons, hawthrons, protons, antiprotons, neutrons, antineutrons, electrons, positrons, among others brings up the debate between the limit of the scientific and the mystical, logic, between being and non-being.

[282] How can these be observed? The Measurement Problem emerges. Measuring the wave becomes a very difficult job. Finding out how the collapse of wave function occurs and the very function of the wave has led to diverse opinions. This difficulty inherent in the very nature of quantum physics is represented by Shrödinger by the mental experiment known as Shrödinger's Cat. Shrödinger's Cat is a critique of the Copenhagen School's position on quantum physics, has similarities with Heisenberg's Principle of Uncertainty, and shows the limitations of the concept of quantum superposition, which brings to light the "obscure" character of natural reality and problems that the scientific method has to face in order to understand a very complex nature. Criticisms of the Copenhagen Interpretation that show the complexity of the world from the perspective of quantum physics have also been made by other mental experiments, such as the Einstein-Podolsky-Rosen Paradox (also known as EPR Paradox) and Wigner's Friend, which can lead to metaphysics in its critique of quantum entanglement and the problem of the idea that consciousness causes collapse. For the study of some of the main proponents of quantum mechanics, together with ancient science, see Heisenberg, Werner. *Physics and Philosophy*. Trad. br. Jorge L. Ferreira. Brasília: University of Brasilia, 1981; HAWKING, Stephen; PENROSE, Roger. *The Nature of Space and Time*. Trad. br. Alberto Luiz da Rocha Barros. Campinas: Papirus, 1997; EINSTEIN, Albert. *Theory of Special and General Relativity*. Trad. br. Carlos Almeida Pereira. Rio de Janeiro: Contraponto Editora, 2012; ARCHIMEDES. *The Works of Archimedes, Including the Method*. Trad. Ing. Thomas Heath. Chicago: Encyclopaedia Britannica, 1952; BOHM, David. *The Totality and the Involved Order*. Trad. br. Cultrix. São Paulo: Editora Cultrix, 1980; PTOLEMY. *The Almagest*. Trad. Ing. C. Taliaferro. Chicago: Encyclopaedia Britannica, 1952.

optimistic.[283] He believed that man could know nature, even if he had preconceptions of it. Quantum mechanics, for its part, recognizes certain epistemic difficulties that the scientific method must offer in the investigation of the natural world – interestingly, quantum mechanics has had important proponents in periods of war and destruction. Second, Bacon had a view of the scientist as an observer, less critical than that of quantum mechanics. Third, the panlogism dreamed by Bacon seems very pretentious to quantum criticism. In the fourth place, the same can be said of the idea that interdisciplinary knowledge will bring social harmony and progress. Fifthly, Baconian induction is, in that context, associated with the idea of overcoming ignorance after the Renaissance and the Reformation, which is a different context. Therefore, Baconian thought does not fit perfectly in quantum mechanics or in classical mechanics.

Although not modern, it was not antithetical to modernity. There were prototypical modern elements in Bacon. There were also elements of quantum mechanics prototypically in Bacon. His ideas were not surpassed by it.[284] Like modern scientists, Bacon was an optimist about the capacity of science.[285] Like quantum scientists,

---

[283] BACON, Francis. *The Advancement of Learning* [1605], p. 145.

[284] The problem of nonlocality and causality present in the particle-particle-wave-particle relationship and in the very concept of wave, which has been studied in quantum physics, seems to contradict Bacon's inductive proposition that the inductivist will arrive at knowledge by discovering the causal nexus between the primary axioms, the intermediates and the endings. However, if one takes into account Bohm's propositions that a strong concept of indeterminacy, nonlocality, and non-causation in quantum physics runs counter to Einstein's General Theory of Relativity, and therefore, in order to escape impasse, the possibility of postulating a program of studies in which there is a medium field theory in which the velocity of a particle does not exceed the speed of light and an idea of space and time in which the zero point of the wave-particle excitation is measured as 10^{-33} cm in a *plenum*, which is a deeper instance of the "unity" of reality – and which differs from empty space, proposed to recover the sense of "totality" in the physical, so tension between the Baconian method and quantum physics can be minimized. See BOHM, David. *The Totality and the Involved Order.* Trad. br. Cultrix. São Paulo: Editora Cultrix. 1980.

[285] Rossi points out: "[There are] two central points of Baconian philosophy: it is necessary to replace the worship of nature with the cult of books and tradition,

he failed to suppress theoretical preconceptions and openness to the mystical, which would aid thinking about method. Like many modern scientists, he wanted to base a whole system of thinking on science. Like quantum scientists, he used assumptions that were not definitely materialistic or mechanistic (in the modern sense of the word) in the practical use of his method. The "moderns" with Bacon wanted to give impetus to a science considered prey to the medieval world and "obscurantism." The "quantum," also with Bacon, wanted to "break" the uncontrolled advance of this science and criticize what had become an "idol."[286] However, all these examples, as has already been said, do not make Bacon a "modern" or a "quantum theorist."

The synthesis of analysis-empirical, language-phenomenon, or world-structure of contemporary philosophy anticipated Bacon. Bacon's criticism of the misuse of language in the idol of the forum—which reverberates in the criticism of other idols—and the importance it gives to the understanding of it and to the necessity of its good use, has been presented in the previous chapter. The fact that he was not only an empirical scientist placed in a position of relevance in the framework of contemporary philosophy, and, more precisely, as a forerunner of important insights must now be explored.[287] For example, if the whole of Bacon's work had been

---

restoring the possibility of fruitful 'conniving with things': the purpose of the 'collection' is not to amuse or arouse curiosity, but to be a means of study, a powerful instrument for the elucidation of scientific research." ROSSI, Paolo. *Francis Bacon: From Magic to Science*, p. 96.

[286] In this case, the idol could be both that of the Theater, because of trust in authority rather than data, as in the Forum, by the transformation of scientific discourse into dialectics, that is, in non-empirical reasoning and language. See BACON, Francis. *Novum Organum*, p. 50.

[287] Logical Positivism, which developed concepts of Analytic Philosophy since Frege, is considered a philosophical school that accepts the empirical model of science. However, for both the analytic philosopher and the logical positivist, the philosopher's function is not to work as an empirical scientist, but rather to analytically define, by the analysis of language, the conditions of the possibility of knowing and the limits of empirical activity itself. The analysis of language would give the empirical scientist support (depending on each philosopher) semantic, syntactic, ontological etc. for his work. It turns out that Logical Positivism rejected several metaphysical categories, considering them meaningless, which Bacon

more emphatically considered by the philosophical tradition, and the English author had been better understood, the idea of the linguistic turnaround, that is, the study of language as a condition of possibility of the empirical work and knowledge of the world, might not have been dated so late. Here is one of his verdicts on the subject:

> In fact, men associate themselves through speech, and words are coined by the common people. And the words, imposed in an improper and inept way, terribly block the intellect. Neither the definitions nor the explanations with which learned men lodge and defend themselves in certain domains restore things to their place. On the contrary, words force the intellect and disturb it completely. And men are thus drawn into countless useless controversies and fantasies.[288]

---

did not do. Hence the fact that certain analysts, such as Ayer (1910-1989), Carnap (1891-1970), and Hempel (1905-1997) had a more materialistic notion of empiria than Bacon. With criticism of Logical Positivism, Analytic Philosophy has some thinkers who have dealt better with the philosophical schools of the European continent—Transcendental Philosophy, Phenomenology, Structuralism, among others—that are more critical of empirical science. Among these authors are Wittgenstein, Sellars (1912-1989), and Kripke (1940-). Wittgenstein, especially in the phase of the *Philosophical Investigations*, also known as the second Wittgenstein phase, was a critic of language as constituted of an essence to be discovered and as a condition of possibility of knowledge, ideas that had been more or less adopted by analytical philosophers, by logical positivists, and by himself in the work *Tractatus Logico-Philosophicus*. Wittgenstein, in *Philosophical Investigations*, maintains that the meaning of a sentence is its use, that different uses of language occur because there are similarities of families between sets of sentences, which differentiate one from the other, as well as language being used as a game, that is, with specific rules aimed at a practical result. It is argued that Wittgenstein breaks with the concept of linguistic turn of philosophy, descending on the descriptive capacity of language itself, and criticizing empirical realism for it to be possible, on the one hand, closer to the phenomenology and, on the other hand, the idea of the death of the subject present in structuralism. Sellars was a critic of what he called the Dice Myth. For him, empiricism did not have sufficient internal coherence to give the investigator certainty that what was "given" by the senses was what he appeared to be. Kripke, by denying the Kantian unity between the transcendental I, the notion that the necessary knowledge is *a priori*, and proposing a form of externalism—influencing Hilary Putnam (1926-2016)—separates mind, language and world, approaching the concepts of structure and phenomena in French and German schools of philosophy.

[288] BACON, Francis. *Novum Organum*, p. 22.

The "discovery of language" would not then be a discovery of mature modern thinkers, within a context in which philosophers no longer possessed the mystical prejudices of the ancient and medieval, but would already be present in philosophy and would not sacrifice the metaphysics, theology, and mysticism for this purpose.[289] The whole theoretical framework that Bacon had, using it as presuppositions

---

[289] Heirs of Kant, Hegel, Romanticism, and Idealism, and contemporary continental European philosophers have established theses and works that seek to fill the imperfections of the thinkers who preceded them. In France, Saussurre (1857-1913), a structuralist, undertook major works on linguistics and semiotics, presenting his own concepts about what signs are and what they are meant. Derrida (1930-2004), influenced by Saussure, sought to unite the study of language and phenomenology, appropriating certain concepts of Husserl (1859-1938), in the work *The Voice and the Phenomenon*. A dialogue between the Derridian work of deconstruction and the hermeneutics of Gadamer (1900-2002) was also attempted. This same spirit of linguistic-phenomenological synthesis is present in other contemporaneous continental European authors, even though post-structuralism, existentialist nihilism, and the philosophical postmodernity is as well. In the concept of *Objective Post-Hegelian Idealism*, by Vittorio Hösle (1960-), the relationship between Structure and Being, by the Brazilian resident in Germany, Lorentz Puntel (1935-), is the *Communicative Act* of the German Jürgen Habermas (1929), the resounding of the tension between Heidegger's language, existence and phenomenon in the philosophies of the Franco-Romanian Cioran (1911-1995), and the Transcendental Pragmatics of the German Karl Otto-Apel (1922-), along with other examples. In addition to developing their own theses, these authors, with exceptions, have absorbed the spirit of the "linguistic turn" or of the "proto-veneer" in order to put the language in evidence, and thus dialogue with Kant's philosophy, with Neokantism and with Hegel under a contemporary prism and approach, at least on a dialogical level, with Analytical or Anglo-Saxon Philosophy. But both they and the Anglo-Saxons, in general, ignore Bacon. Even Descartes, with his mind-body dualism, has more support in a wing of contemporary philosophy, the Philosophy of Mind, than Bacon. It turns out that the post-metaphysical spirit and linguistic post-turnaround of some of these authors led them to consider empiria as an activity proper to the empirical and non-philosophical sciences or to phenomenology and idealism schools not well elaborated before the modern or analysis of language as a function of the philosopher in dialogue with the (empirical) scientists. Bacon thus came to be seen as an author who 1) either had no relevant thesis on language, 2) or could not undergo the same revisions that the metaphysicians of the past suffered for contemporaries because he was not a metaphysician, but an empirical one, 3) or should be remembered as a modern proto-scientist and not a philosopher in the full sense. However, all the study in these chapters shows that this view of Bacon is wrong.

to interpret nature and even to define the word "nature," places him in a position in which there is a certain discontinuity between the common language (of the forum) and things spoken, which includes nature itself. According to Bacon, "language," understood in the ordinary and ordinary sense, did not know nature itself. The inductive method would then also be a metalanguage effort, a critical research on language. Hence the possibility that Bacon's "analytic philosophy" is as much a part of empirical science as empirical science is part of "analytic philosophy", since there is no "analysis" in the full sense without the method and there is no method with the idol of the (linguistic) forum. In a way, the method needs the language, and the language needs the method. Take, for example, the doctor William Harvey (1578-1657), famous for the study of blood circulation. This presents a sample of how language can give different meaning to things. He says that the name "spirits" was given to "spaces" or "vacuums" in the veins, arteries, nerves, etc. Now, even if "spirits" could mean nothing but the sensible, that name alone would attract the scientific study of metaphysics, mysticism, and religion. Thus, it is seen that not only observation but the naming of what is observed is an essential part of the realm of reality.[290] Viewed from this angle, the very concept of empiria in Bacon is not antagonistic to phenomenology,[291] as those who classify it as a pre-critical empiricist (as Popper) want, since Bacon's

---

[290] "Fernelius (1497-1558), and many others, suppose that there are aereal spirits and invisible substances. Fernelius proves that there are animal spirits, by saying that the cells in the brain are apparently unoccupied, and the nature abhors a vacuum, he concludes that in the living body they are filled with spirits, just as Erasistratus (304-250 BC) had held, because the arteries were empty of blood, therefore they must be filled with spirits. But medical schools admit three kinds of spirits: the natural spirits flowing through the veins, the vital spirits through the arteries, and the animal spirits through the nerves; whence physicians say, out of Galen, sometimes the parts of the brain are oppressed by sympathy, because the faculty of the essence, i. e., the spirit, is overwhelmed: and sometimes this happens independently of the essence." Harvey, William. *On Circulation of the Blood*, p. 316.

[291] Bacon's criticism of the dialectic, which "only in name has relation to what it proposes," would then be a criticism of language, as well as the poor study of natural phenomena, a problem whose language is included as a determining factor. See Ibid., p. 50.

language is both strictly empirical and imbued with a mystical critique of itself and its inherent limits. If Bacon had gained greater influence among the moderns, perhaps the dichotomy between empirical science and philosophy, as well as the distinction between English-speaking philosophy and continental philosophy, would not be accentuated. Both empirical science and phenomenology are united in the English philosopher. It is the resource of language that he uses to simultaneously speak of nature as a homogeneous entity, his exact knowledge, and the inability of man to know a single being, however small, without a meticulous process elaborated in the inductive method. It was necessary to go beyond the limits of words. The proposition of the mathematical language of reality would even imply an overcoming of the limits between what is said about the thing and the thing itself, or between what appears from the thing and is captured by language and the reliable description of the real. These facts make any attitude that relegates Bacon to the history of induction[292] of modern science unrelated[293] to contemporary philosophy unsustainable. Rather, a revision of Bacon's legacy must be realized, so that his real contributions to contemporary philosophy are known and valued.

5.3 Concessions and Critical Appraisal

At the end of any exposition on Bacon, it might seem implausible to the academy's view that no criticism should be given to the English philosopher as plausible.

The realization that Bacon is a thinker full of idiosyncrasies does not negate the need for a greater understanding of this issue.[294] In fact, there are concessions to be made to this criticism.

- First, it must be conceded that Bacon was confused in articulating his ideas.

---

[292] BACON, Francis. *Novum Organum* [1620], pp. 15, 21.

[293] BACON, Francis. *The Advancement of Learning* [1605], pp. 140-150.

[294] As seen in the fourth chapter, even current theories that try to unite modern and contemporary thinking, such as the General Systems Theory and Epistemology of Systems Thinking, are not the same as Bacon's thought.

- Secondly, it must be conceded that he may not have been aware of the logical consequences of everything he articulated philosophically.
- Thirdly, it must be conceded that this lack of synthesis and the excess of paradoxes in his thinking contributed to the misunderstanding of his ideas and made him, in a way, guilty of the criticisms made of him.

All this, however, does not contradict the previous chapters, nor does it measure forces with the preceding sections, which are critical of the reading of Bacon by empirical science and the philosophical academy. In addition, the central thesis of all the chapters, that the proposal of Baconian science (*Instauratio Magna*) had a mystical influence, sometimes from the mystery schools, at other times stemming from a peculiar theologization of Christianity, remains untouched.

To finalize this, a final synthesis[295] will be made, as follows:

1. Bacon was mystical, but experimentally methodical;
2. He was an inductivist, but also a critical philosopher of language and the use of logic;
3. He theologized the method and the cosmos, but was also a critic of the old superstitions;
4. He emphasized the discourse on technique, on the new and on progress, but also used old, non-inductive, and even metaphysical assumptions;
5. He criticized Plato and Aristotle, but did not break completely with the two;
6. He focused his work on the discourse on science, but saw it as a sort of redemptive priesthood of all social life;
7. He was misunderstood, but also did not avoid paradoxes between the clear inductive method and the complex use of

---

[295] Although Bacon has not been very synthetic in his articulations and ten points are not sufficient for an ideal synthesis of his thought, this synthesis will help to understand what has been said so far.

theological, mystical, and deductive insights and concepts in dialogue with the method;

8. He was not a modern scientist, but also not an antithesis to one;
9. He did not fit completely into quantum mechanics, but also has points in common with it;
10. He did not possess all the central concerns of contemporary philosophy, but he has already anticipated the critique of language and the spirit of empirical or linguistic-phenomenological synthesis in it.

6.

CONCLUSION

THIS WORK INVESTIGATED THE MYSTICAL FOUNDATIONS OF the science of Francis Bacon. Hermetic elements, esoteric symbolism, Anglican and Puritan religiosity, among other aspects by which mysticism was rooted in Bacon's thought, were studied. The inductive method was treated in itself, that is, as separate from any external influence, as if interacting with the mystic. Baconian science, even when investigated in the rigor of the method itself, has proved to be contradictory and full of gaps here. Such gaps were fulfilled by the mystical presuppositions of the English philosopher. Indeed, as seen, this influence on the science of Bacon was an important factor for understanding the reasons why he gave science so great a mission for humanity. It has also been shown that it is the influence of the mystical that provides the key to understanding the real aspect of Bacon's rejection and acceptance of the ancients, especially of Aristotle and Plato. Bacon was thus presented under a different light from that in which he appears only as the philosopher of method or even as the father of modern science. He was seen as a complex thinker, but one whose complexity was needed to be taken seriously. The easiest way to avoid the paradoxes and to reduce it to the inductive method was rejected. This reductionism was even considered as harmful to the knowledge of Bacon's ideas. Baconian science itself came to be observed without taking into account the anachronism of the gaze already affected by the materialism of modernity so that the philosopher who at first glance rejected any "idol" on his method was also framed in the category of mysticism.

The study did not pretend to exhaust the theme that it considered. Some issues were left open; others were vigorously defended. For example, while the central thesis of this work was strongly defended, the investigation of the degrees of reception of the ancients (especially of Aristotle and Plato), as well as of the relation between Bacon and scientific ideas that were born in the so-called postmodern era, served more as an opening for a fruitful debate. These four chapters have shown that Bacon was not an intrinsically modern author and that, yes, the old world and the postmodern or contemporary era is more influenced by Bacon than is currently imagined. However, the major purpose was to reveal this fact: that Bacon's science, grounded in mysticism, is not intrinsically modern, nor intrinsically opposed to ancient thinkers, but is an opening for interpretations favorable to Bacon's work by contemporary scientists and scholars of ancient thought. In this way, Bacon's legacy is revitalized. The new facets of Bacon presented demand a new academic treatment of the author. This legacy unites the English philosopher with an empirical science of philosophy and provides the spiritual and the religious with the opportunity to contribute to the academic debate without being pre-empted as anti-scientific, given the very concept of science (if understood as averse to mysticism) has been questioned.

The Western world has classified much of what is considered philosophical, metaphysical, and scientific in the Eastern world as superstition, pantheism, and pseudoscience. For that, they have the support of academics from various areas. In Bacon's case, as discussed, there is the possibility of thinking of the method as having non-modern rather than completely Western presuppositions – if modernity and Western thought are taken in the opposite sense of the mystical and the notion of the non-mechanical world. Certainly, the question addressed was not intended to make Bacon an Eastern thinker, nor to study him in this light, but to show that there is a way in which science can be understood without absolutely modern parameters, and in which there is not a biased rejection of everything that does not fit this model as unscientific. The paradoxes of his statements were not hidden. Rather, they were expounded to strengthen the thesis that the Baconian mentality still did not function mechanically and possessed intuitions of a pre-modern world so credible to the author that they did not seem paradoxical to the method. Bacon is not just the father of modern science, but a thinker who has left open the possibilities of creating a new world, a world certainly not equivalent to modernity. At a time when modernity is being overcome by postmodernity, Bacon is an indispensable thinker for the academic world.

REFERENCES

ADORNO; HORKEIMER. *Dialética do Esclarecimento*. Trad. br. Guido Antônio de Almeida. Rio de Janeiro: Zahar, 2006.

AGRIPPA, Cornelius. *Three Books of Occult Philosophy - Book I*. USA: Hermetics, 2000.

_____, Cornelius. *Três Livros de Filosofia Religiosa*. Trad. br. Marcos Malvezzi. São Paulo: Madras, 2008.

ALTHUSIUS, Johannes. *Política*. Trad. br, Joubert de Oliveira Brízida. Rio de Janeiro: Topbooks Editora, 2003.

AMARAL, Roberto; SANTOS, Ângela. Revista Vozes dos Vales. *O Eros como conhecimento: uma leitura de O Banquete de Platão*. Minas Gerais, N° 2, Ano 1, 10/2012.

ANDREAE, Valentin. *Christianopolis*. New York: Oxford University Press, 1916.

APHRODISIAS, Alexander. *On the Soul Part I: Soul as the Form of the Body, Parts of the Soul, Nourishment and Perception*. Translated by Victor Carlson., New York: Bloomsbury, 2014.

ARCHIMEDES. *The Works of Archimedes, Including the Method*. Trad. Ing. Thomas Heath. Chicago: Encyclopaedia Britannica, 1952.

ARISTOTLE. *Arte Retórica e Arte Poética*. Trad. br. Antônio Pinto de CARVALHO. Rio de Janeiro: Editora Ediouro – Tecnoprint, 1979.

_____, *Categorias*. Trad. br. Maria José Figueiredo. Lisboa: Instituto Piaget, 2000

_____, *De Anima*. Trad. pt. Carlos Humberto Gomes. Lisboa: Edições 70, 2001.

_____, *Ética a Nicômaco*. Tradução br. Pietro Nassetti. São Paulo: Editora Matins Claret, 2006.

_____, *Física I e II*. Trad. br. Lucas Angioni. Campinas: Editora da Unicamp. 2009.

_____, *Metafísica*. Tradução br. Marcelo Perine. São Paulo: Edições Loyola, 2002.

_____, *Organon III: Analíticos Anteriores*. Trad. br. Pinharanda Gomes. Lisboa: Guimarães Editores, 1986.

_____, *Organon IV: Analíticos Posteriores*. Trad. br. Pinharanda Gomes. Lisboa: Guimarães Editores, 1987.

_____, *Política*. Trad. br. Mário da Gama Cmy. 3. Brasília: EDUNB, 1997.

ASCLEPIUS. *Corpus Hermeticum – Tome II*. Paris: Societè D'Edition a Les Belles Lettres, 1945.

BACON, Francis. *A Sabedoria dos Antigos*. Trad. br. Gilson César Cardoso de Souza. São Paulo: UNESP, 2002.

_____, Francis. *Ensaios sobre Moral e Política*. Trad. br. Edson Bini. Bauru-SP: EDIPRO, 2001.

_____, Francis. *Essays*. Nebraska: Project Gutenberg, 2003.

_____, Francis. *Novum Organum [1620]*. Trad. br. José Aluysio Reis de Andrade. São Paulo: Abril Cultural, 1984.

_____, Francis. *O progresso do conhecimento*. Trad. br. Raul Fiker. São Paulo, UNESP, 2007.

_____, Francis. *Nova Atlândida [1624]*. Trad. br. José Aluysio Reis de Andrade. São Paulo: Abril Cultural, 1984.

_____, Francis. *The Letters and Life of Francis Bacon Including All His Occasional Works*. Londres, J. SPPEDING (Ed.), 1890-1895, 7 V.

_____, Francis. *The works of Francis Bacon*. London: Ed. Sppeding-Ellis- Heat, 1859.

_____, Francis. *Works (Philosophical works)*. Reprinted from the texts and translations of Ellis and Sppeding. London: Edited by John M. Robertson, 1905.

_____, Francis. *The works of Francis Bacon.* Londres, R. LELLIS; J. SPPEDING; D. D. HEAT (Ed.), 14 V., 1963.

BAXTER, James. *The Greatest of Literary Problems, the Authorship of the Shakespeare Works; An Exposition of All the Points at Issue, from Their Inception to the Present Moment.* London: Forgotten Books, 2015.

BOTVINA, Renata. *Francis Bacon's Natural Philosophy as Natural Language.* Brasil: Studies in Logic, Grammar and Rethoric, 8, 21, 2005.

BARREIRO, Mateus; CARVALHO, Alonso. *Dimensão Ética e Epistemológica: as Contribuições de Aristóteles para a Formação Humana na Atualidade.* Marília-SP, REGRAD, UNIVEM V. 8, N° 1, pp. 122-138, 2015.

BIRUNI, Al. *As Características dos Planetas.* Trad. br. Magus Occultus. Editor Brasil: Magus Oculltus, 2006.

BOHM, David. *A Totalidade e a Ordem Implicada.* Trad. br. Cultrix. São Paulo: Editora Cultrix, 1980.

BOMBASSARO, Luiz Carlos. *As fronteiras da epistemologia: como se produz o conhecimento.* Vozes: Petrópoles-RJ, 1992.

BRADSHAW, David. *Aristotle East and West.* Cambridge: Cambridge University Press, 2004.

BRUNO, Giordano. *De La Magia de lós Vínculos em General.* Traducción Ezequiel Gatto. Buenos Aires: Editorial Cactus, 2007.

BULTMANN, Rudolf. *Crer e Compreender.* Trad. br. Altmann, Schlupp e Shneider. São Leopoldo: Editora Sinodal, 1987.

BURCKHARDT, Titus. *Alquimia.* Brasil: Editora Dom Quixote, 1991.

CATTANEI, Elisabetta. *Entes Matemáticos e Metafísica: Platão, a Academia e Aristóteles em confronto.* Trad. br. Fernando S. Moreira. São Paulo: Edições Loyola, 2005.

CASSIN, Barbara. *Aristóteles e o lógos: contos da fenomenologia comum.* São Paulo-SP: Loyola, 1999.

CHALMERS, Alan. *O que é ciência, afinal?* Trad. br. Raul Fiker. São Paulo: Editora Brasiliense, 1993.

CHINCHILLA, Anastasio. *Anales Historicos de La Medicina em General.* Valencia:

Imprensa de Lopez Y Compania, 1841.

COMTE, Augusto. *Catecismo Positivista*. Trad. br. José Arthur Giannotti e Miguel Lemos. São Paulo: Nova Cultural, 1991.

_____, Augusto. *Curso de Filosofia Positivista*. Trad. br. José Arthur Giannotti e Miguel Lemos. São Paulo: Nova Cultural, 1991.

_____, Augusto. *Discurso Preliminar sobre o Conjunto do Positivo*. Trad. br. José Arthur Giannotti e Miguel Lemos. São Paulo: Nova Cultural, 1991.

COPENHAVER, Brian. *Hermetica*. Cambridge: Cambridge University Press, 2002.

_____, Brian. *Magic in Western Culture*. New York: Cambridge University Press, 2015.

COPERNICUS, Nicolaus. *On the Revolution of Heavenly Spheres*. Trad. Ing. Charles G. Wallis. Chicago: Encyclopaedia Britannica, 1952.

CORNFORD, Francis. *La Filosofia no Escrita, y Otros Ensayos*. Barcelona: Editora Ariel, 1974.

_____, Francis. *Platón y Parménides*. Madrid: Visor Dis., S. A., 1989.

CORRIGAN, Kevin. *Plotinus' Theory of Matter-Evil and the Question of Substance: Plato, Aristotle, and Alexander of Aphrodisias*. Leuven: Peeters, 1995.

COSTA, Marcos. *O Uno e o Múltiplo na Cosmologia de Plotino*. Pernambuco, Revista Symposium, Ano 3, Edição Especial, 1999.

COULANGES. Fustel. *A Cidade Antiga*. Trad. br. Fernando de Aguiar. São Paulo: Martins Fontes, 1995.

COULIANO, Ioan. *Eros and Magic in Renaissance*. Translated to English by Margaret Cook. London: University Chicago Press, 1987.

CULVERWELL, Nathaniel. *An Elegant and Learned Discourse of the Light of Nature*. Indianapolis: Libert Fund, 2001.

CUSA, Nicolau. *A douta ignorância*. Trad. br. Reinholdo Aluysio Ullman. Edipcurs, 2002.

DARWIN, Charles. *On the Origin of the Species*. Chicago: Encyclopaedia Britannica, 1952.

DAWSON, Christopher. *A Formação da Cristandade: Das Origens na Tradição Judaico-cristã à Ascensão e Queda da Unidade Medieval*. Trad. br. Márcia Xavier de Brito. São Paulo: É Realizações, 2014.

DAVA. *Um céu mais que perfeito: como Copérnico revolucionou o Cosmos*. Trad. br. Ana Cláudia Ferrari. São Paulo: Companhia das Letras, 2015.

DEE, John. *The Rosicrucian Secrets*. England: K. Q. M. 1997.

DESCARTES, René. *O Discurso do Método*. Trad. br. Ciro Mioranza. São Paulo-SP: Escala Educacional, 2006.

DHANANI, Alnoor. *The Physical Theory of Kalam*. New York: E. J. Brill, 1994.

DIDEROT, Denis. *Textos Escolhidos*. Trad. br. Marilena Chiauí. São Paulo: Abril Cultural, 1985.

DOROTHEA, Krook. *Two Baconians: Robert Boyle and Joseph Glanvill*. Huntington: Huntington Library Quarterly, 1955.

DYER, Colin. *O Simbolismo na Maçonaria*. Trad. br. Sérgio Cernea. São Paulo: Madras, 2006.

DUNCA, Petru. *The Perspective of the Analytic Philosophy of Religion on the Almightiness of Gods and the Status of Evil in the Religions of the Ancient Near East, Mesopotamia and Egypt*. European Journal of Science and Theology, Vol. 8, Nº 3, 2012, 27-35.

DURANT, Will. *A Filosofia de Francis Bacon*. Trad. br. Maria Theresa Miranda. , Rio de Janeiro: Edições de Ouro,1964.

EINSTEIN, Albert. *Teoria da Relatividade Especial e Geral*. Trad. br. Carlos Almeida Pereira. Rio de Janeiro: Contraponto Editora, 2012.

ELIADE, Mircea. *Ferreiros e Alquimistas*. Trad. pt. Carlos Pessoa. Lisboa: Relógio D'água, 1987.

ELLIS, Brian. *The Philosophy of Nature: The Guide to the New Essentialism*. Chesham: Acumen, 2002.

EPICURO. *Antologia de Textos*. Trad. br. Agostinho da Silva. São Paulo: Abril Cultural, 1980.

EUCLIDES. *The Thirteen Books of Euclid's Elements*. Trad. Ing. Thomas Heath. Chicago: Encyclopaedia Britannica, 1952.

EVOLA, Julius. *A Tradição Hermética*. Trad. br. Maria Teresa Simões. São Paulo: Colecção Esfinge-Edições 70, 1971.

FARRINGTON, Benjamin. *The Philosophy of Francis Bacon*. Illinois: University Chicago Press. 1966.

FERNANDES, Edrisi. *Antecedentes Histórico-Filosóficos da Problemática do Bem e do Mal no Freiheitsschrift de Schelling: Aproximações Gnósticas*. Natal: UFRN-Tese de Doutorado, 2010.

FICINO, Marsilio. *Platonic Theology – Vol. 1*. USA: Harvard University Press, 2001.

_____, Marsilio. *Platonic Theology – Vol. II*. USA: Harvard University Press, 2002.

_____, Marsilio. *Platonic Theology – Vol. III*. USA: Harvard University Press, 2003.

_____, Marsilio. *Platonic Theology – Vol. IV*. USA: Harvard University Press, 2004.

_____, Marsilio. *Platonic Theology – Vol. V*. USA: Harvard University Press, 2005.

_____, Marsilio. *Platonic Theology – Vol. VI*. USA: Harvard University Press, 2006.

FIKER, Raul. *O conhecer e o saber em Francis Bacon*. São Paulo: Nova Alexandria, 1996.

FLUDD, Robert. *Life and Writings*. Kirkwall: William Peace and Son, Kirkwall, 1902.

GALEN. *On the Natural Faculties*. Trad. Ing. Arthur J. Brock. Chicago: Encyclopaedia Britannica, 1952.

GALILEU. *Dialogues Concerning the Two New Sciences*. Trad. Ing. H. Crew and A. de Salvio. Chicago: Encyclopaedia Britannica, 1980.

_____, *Ciência e Fé: Cartas de Galileu sobre o Acordo do Sistema Copernicano com a Bíblia*. Trad. br. Carlos Arthur Nascimento. São Paulo: UNESP, 2009.

GALVÃO, Roberto Carlos Simões. *Francis Bacon: teoria, método e contribuições para a educação*. Florianópolis, R. Inter. Interdisc. interthesis, v.4, jul. /dez. 2007.

GILBERT, William. *On the Loadstone and Magnetic Bodies.* P. F. Mottelay. Chicago: Encyclopaedia Britannica, 1980.

GROARKE, Louis. *An Aristotelian Account of Induction: Creating Something from Nothing.* Ontario: McGill-Queen's University Press, 2009.

GUENÓN, René. *Considerações sobre a Iniciação.* Trad. br. Igor Silva. São Paulo: IRGET, 1946.

_____, René. *Símbolos fundamentais da ciência sagrada.* Trad. br. Luiz Pontual. São Paulo: IRGET, 2011.

HAMMOND, Debora. *The Science of Sinthesis: Exploring the Social Implications of General Systems Theory.* Colorado: University Press Colorado, 2010.

HARVEY, William. *An Anatomical Distinction on the Motion of the Heart and Blood in Animals.* Trad. Ing. Robert Willis. Chicago: Encyclopaedia Britannica, 1980.

HAWKING, Stephen; PENROSE, Roger. *A Natureza do Espaço e Tempo.* Trad. br. Alberto Luiz da Rocha Barros. CamPinas: Papirus, 1997.

HEISENBERG, Werner. *Física e Filosofia.* Trad. br. Jorge L. Ferreira. Brasília: Universidade de Brasília, 1981.

HILL, Christopher. *O mundo de ponta cabeça: ideias radicais durante a Revolução Inglesa de 1640.* Trad. br. Renato Janine Ribeiro. São Paulo: Companhia das Letras, 1987.

HIPPOCRATIC. *Writings.* Trad. Ing. Francis Adams. Chicago: Encyclopaedia Britannica, 1952.

HOFSTADTER, Richard. *Social Darwinism in America Thought.* Boston: Beacon Press, 1992.

HOOYKAAS, Reijer. *A religião e o desenvolvimento da ciência moderna.* Trad. br. Fernando Dídimo Viveira. Brasília: UNB, 1988.

HUIZINGA, Johan. *O Outono da Idade Média.* Trad. br. Francis Petra Janssen. São Paulo: Cosac Naify, 2013.

HUME, David. *Uma investigação sobre o entendimento humano.* Trad. br. José de Almeida Marques. São Paulo: UNESP, 1999.

IAMBLICUS. *De Anima.* Translated by John F. Finamore. Boston: Brill, 2002.

INCOGNTO, Magus. *The Secret of Rosacrucian Symbols*. Chicago: Advanced Thought Publishing CO., 2008.

JAPIASSU, Hilton. *Francis Bacon: O profeta da ciência moderna*. São Paulo: Letras e Letras, 1995.

JONAS, Hans. *La Religion Gnostica: El mensaje del Dios Extraño y los comienzos del cristianismo*. Traducción de Menchu Gutiérrez. Madrid: Ediciones Siruela, 2003.

JONES, Marie; FIAXMAN, Larry. *Viral Mythology: How the Truth of the Ancients was Encoded and Passed Down*. USA: The Career Press, 2014.

JÚNIOR, João; REDYSON, Deyve. *Platão e o papel do Demiurgo na geração da vida cósmica*. Paraíba, Religare 7 (1), pp. 72-80, 2010.

KEMPER, Érico. *A Inserção de Tópicos de Astronomia no Estudo da Mecânica em Uma Abordagem Epistemológica*. Rio Grande do Sul, v. 18 n. 3, Instituto de Física-UFRGS, 2007.

KEPLER, Johannes. *The Harmony of the World*. Trad. Ing. Charles G. Wallis. Chicago: Encyclopaedia Britannica, 1952.

KIECKHEFER, Richard. *La Magia en La Edad Media*. Traducción Montserrat Cabré. Barcelona: Editorial Crítica, 1992.

KINGSLEY, Peter. *Filosofía Antigua, Misterios y Magia*. Traducción Alejandro Coroleu. Atalanta: Girona, 1995.

KUHN, Thomas. *A estrutura das revoluções científicas*. Trad. br. Beatriz Viana Boeira e Nelson Boeira. São Paulo: Perspectiva, 2007.

LEVI, Eliphas. *Dogma e Ritual de Alta Magia*. Trad. A. E. Waite. Brasil: Benjamim Rwe, 2001.

LIÃO, Ireneu de. *Contra as Heresias*. Trad. br. L. Costa. São Paulo: Paulus Editora, 1995.

LOUTH, Andrew. *The Origins of the Christian Mystical Tradition: From Plato to Denys*. New York: Oxford University Press, 2007.

LUCRÉCIO. *Da Natureza*. Trad. br. Agostinho da Silva. São Paulo: Abril Cultural, 1980.

LUKASIEWICZ, Jan. *Aristotle's Sillogistic: From the Standpoint of the Modern*

Formal Logic. Oxford: Oxford University Press, 1951.

MACEDO, Cecília. *O Neoplatonismo e o Aristotelismo no Hilemorfismo Universal de Ibne Gabirol (Avicebron)*. Porto Alegre, Veritas, V. 52, N° 3, pp. 132-148, 2007.

MALINOWSKI, Bronislaw. *Magia, Ciencia y Religión*. Traducción António Prez Ramos. Espana: Planeta-Agostini, 1948.

MANZO, Silvia. *Francis Bacon y el atomismo: una nueva evaluación*. São Paulo, Scientia Studia, vol. 6, Outubro/Dezembro, 2008.

McKNIGHT, Stephen A. *The Religious Foundations of Francis Bacon's Thought*. Columbia: University of Missouri Press, 2006.

McLUHAN, Eric. *Francis Bacon's Theory of Communication and Media*. Toronto: McLuhan Studies, Issue 4, 1999.

MANUEL, Frank. *El pensamiento utópico em El mundo occidental*. Madri: Tauros, 1981.

MARQUES, Hélio Morais. *O Domínio da Vida*. Ordem Rosacruz, Curitiba-Pr, 2009.

MATHERS, Macgregor. *The Kabbalah Unveiled*. New York: The Theosophical Publishing Company of New York, 1912.

MANZO, Silvia. *Francis Bacon y el atomismo: una nueva evaluación*. São Paulo: Scientia Studia, vol. 6, Outubro/Dezembro, 2008.

MORAIS, Regis. *Filosofia, Educação e Sociedade: ensaios filosóficos*. Campinas: Papirus, 1989.

MORE, Thomas. *A Utopia*. Trad. br. Luis de Andrade. São Paulo: Abril Cultural, 1997.

NEWMAN. *The Politics of Aristotle. With Introduction, Two Prefatory Essays and Critical and Explanatory Notes*. Oxford: Clarendon Press, 1902.

NORTH. *The Six Day of Creation and Francis Bacon's Great Instauration: Sacred Creativity and the Six Days Work in Bacon*. England, Francis Bacon Society, Baconiana, Volume 1, No. 3, 2009.

NYORD, Rune; RYHOLT. Kim. *Lotus and Laurel – Studies on Egyptian Language and Religion in Honor to John Frandsen*. Copenhagen: Museum Tusculanum Press and CNI Publications, 2015.

OLIVEIRA, Manfredo. Ética e racionalidade moderna. São Paulo: Loyola, 1993.

_____, Bernardo Jefferson. *Francis Bacon e a fundamentação da ciência como tecnologia*. Belo Horizonte: UFMG, 2002.

PACKER, James. *Entre os Gigantes de Deus- Uma visão puritana da vida cristã [1991]*. São José dos Campos: Fiel, 1996.

PARACELSO. *Plantas Mágicas*. Trad. br. Attílio Cancian. São Paulo: Hemus Editora, 1976.

PASQUALIN, Camila. *Repressão das práticas curativas tradicionais na primeira modernidade*. Curitiba: UFPR, 2007.

PELTONEN, Markku. *The Cambridge Companion to Bacon*. Cambridge: Cambridge University Press, 2006.

PELUSO, Luis Alberto. *Ética e Utilitarismo*. Campinas: Alínea, 1998.

PHILIPPE Marie-Dominique. *Introdução à Filosofia de Aristóteles*. Trad. br. Gabriel Hibon Bernôni Lemos. São Paulo: Paulus, 2002.

PLATÃO. *O Banquete*. Pará de Minas-MG: Versão Acrópole, 2003.

_____, *República*. Trad. de Maria Helena da Rocha Pereira. Lisboa: Gulbenkian, 1983.

_____, *Timeu-Crítias*. Trad. br. Rodolfo Lopes. Coimbra: CECH, 2011.

PLATTES, Gabriel. *A description of the famous kingdom of Macaria*. London: Francis Constable Edition, 1641.

PLOTINO. *Eneadas I, II e III*. Traduzido por João Baracat Júnior. Tese de Doutorado- Dissertação - Pró-Reitoria de Pesquisa e Pós-Graduação, UNICAMP, Campinas, 2006.

POLITO, Antony. *A Metafísica e a Física de Aristóteles*. Brasília, Physicae Organum, Vol. 1., N. 2, 2015.

POPPER, Karl. *Conjecturas e Refutações*. Trad. br. Sérgio Bath. Brasília: UNB, 1972.

PORFÍRIO. *Isagoge- Introdução às Categorias de Aristóteles*. Traduzido por Pinharada Gomes. Lisboa: Guimarães Editores, 1994.

PORTER, Martin. *Windows of the Soul: Physiognomy in European Culture 1470-1780*. New York: Oxford University Press, 2005.

POTT, Mrs. Henry. *Francis Bacon and His Secret Society*. Chicago: J. Schult and Company, 1891.

PRIBBLE. Paula. *Poetic and Francis Bacon's Ambivalence Toward Language*. Minnesota: St. Cloud State University - Educational Resources Information Center, 1986.

PTOLEMY. *The Amagest*. Trad. Ing. C. Taliaferro. Chicago: Encyclopaedia Britannica, 1952.

PROCLUS. *Commentary on the Timaeus of Plato: Books 1-5*. Translated by Thomas Taylor. USA: Edited by Martin Euser, 2010.

ROBERTSON, John. *The Philosophical Works of Francis Bacon*. New York: Routlegde, 2011.

ROHDEN, Luciana. *Sobre as Causas em Aristóteles*. Porto Alegre, PUCRS, Intuitio, V. 2-No. 1, 2009.

ROSSI, Paolo. *Francis Bacon: da magia à ciência*. Trad. br. Aurora Fornoni Bernadini. Londrina: Eduel, 2006.

ROSSI, Paolo. *A ciência e filosofia dos modernos*. Trad. br. Álvaro Lorencini. São Paulo: UNESP, 1992.

_____, Paolo. *A chave universal: Artes da memorização e lógica combinatória desde Lúlio até Leibnz*. Trad. br. Antonio Angonese. Bauru-SP: EDUSC, 2004.

_____, Paolo. *Naufrágios sem espectador: A ideia do progresso*. Trad. br. Álvaro Lorencini. São Paulo: UNESP, 2000.

_____, Paolo. *O nascimento da ciência moderna na Europa*. Trad. br. Antonio Angonese. Bauru-SP: EDUSC, 2001.

ROUANET, Sérgio Paulo. *As razões do iluminismo*. São Paulo: Companhia das letras, 1987.

ROVERTS, James Deotis. *From Puritanism to Platonism in Seventeenth Century England*. Netherlands: The Hague, 1968.

SECCO, Márcio. *Verdade e método em Francis Bacon*. Dissertação de Mestrado-

Pró-Reitoria de Pesquisa e Pós-Graduação, Universidade Federal de Santa Catarina, Florianópolis, 2004.

SOARES, Guilherme. *O Filósofo e o Éthos Político na República de Platão*. Dissertação de Mestrado- Pró-Reitoria de Pesquisa e Pós-Graduação, UFSM, Santa Maria, 2015.

SONIA, Vanni Rovighi. *História da Filosofia Moderna-da revolução científica a Hegel*. Trad. br Marcos Bagno e Silvana Cobucci Leite. São Paulo: Loyola, 1999.

SHACKELFORD, Jole. *Paracelsianism and the Orthodox Lutheran Rejection of Vital Philosophy in Early Seventeenth-Century Denmark*. USA, Early Science and Medicine, Vol. 8, No. 3, 2003.

SCHOLEM, Gershom. *A Cabala e seu Simbolismo*. Trad. br. Hans Borger. São Paulo: Editora Perspectiva. 997.

SHAW, Gregory. *Theurgy and the Soul: The Neoplatonism of Imablichus*. Pennsylvania: The Pennsylvania State University Press, 1995.

SHLENZINGER, Aharon. *Enigmas y Misterios del Talmud y La Cábala*. Barcelona: Ediciones Obelisco, 2009.

SILVA, Sandro. *A Ética das Virtudes de Aristóteles*. Dissertação de Mestrado – Pró-Reitoria de Pesquisa e Pós-Graduação, Unisinos, São Leopoldo, 2008.

_____, Fernando. *Sobre a Indução em Francis Bacon*. Paraná, *Revista Urutágua-Revista acadêmica multidisciplina DSC/UEM*, nº 14, 2008.

SMITH, Wolfgang. *Ciência e Mito*. Trad. br. Pedro Cava. Campinas: Vide Editorial, 2008.

_____, Wolfgand. *The Wisdow of the Ancient Cosmology*. Oakton: Foundation of Traditional Studies, 2004.

STILLMANN, Robert. *The New Philosophy and Universal Languages in Seventeenth-Century England: Bacon, Hobbes, and Wilkins*. Linguistic Society of America, Vol. 74, No. 2, 1998, USA, pp. 370-372.

STRAUSS, Leo. *Plato's Republic*. Chicago: University of Chicago, 1957.

_____, Leo. *Estudios de Filosofía Política Platónica*. Traducción Amelia Aguado. Buenos Aires: Amorrortu Editores, 2008.

TAYLOR, Charles. *Sources of the Self: The Making of the Modern Identity*.

Cambridge: Cambridge University Press, 1998.

TOV, David Ben Yom. *Hebrew Medical Astrology.* Translation Gerrit Bos. United States: American Philosophical Society, 2011.

WANG, Xiaona. *Francis Bacon's Magic and the Universal Principle of Gravitation.* Francis Bacon Society, Baconiana, Volume 1, N° 6, England, 2009.

WEBSTER, Nestar. *Secret Societies and Subversive Movements.* London: Eworld Inc., 2014.

WEEKS, Sophie. *Francis Bacon's Science of Magic.* Leeds: University of Leeds, 2007.

WIGSTON, W. F. C. *Bacon, Shakespeare and the Rosicrucians.* London: Tübner and Co., 1884.

WOORTMANN, Klaas. *Religião e ciência no Renascimento.* Brasília: UNB, 1997.

VALDEMARIN, Vera Teresa. *Estudando as Lições das Coisas: análise dos fundamentos filosóficos do Método de Ensino Intuitivo.* Campinas: Autores Associados, 2004.

VICKERS, Brian. *Essential Articles for the Study of Francis Bacon.* Hamden: Conn., Archon Books, 1968.

VIEIRA, Raymundo. *Raízes Históricas da Medicina Ocidental.* São Paulo; Editora Fap-Unifesp, 2012.

VINDEX. *Protestants and Freemansory.* USA: Kessinger Publishing, LLC, 2010.

YATES, Francis. *O Iluminismo Rosa-Cruz.* Trad. br. Syomara Cajado. São Paulo: Cultrix-Pensamento, 1992.

_____, Francis. *The Hermetic Tradition in Renaissance Science.* Baltimore: John Hopkins University Press, 1967.

ZATERKA, Luciana. *A filosofia experimental na Inglaterra do século XVIII: Francis Bacon e Robert Boyle.* São Paulo: FAPESP, 2004.

_____, Luciana. *A Longevidade segundo a concepção de vida de Francis Bacon.* Filosofia e História da Biologia, volume 5, número 1, Brasil, 2010.

www.ingramcontent.com/pod-product-compliance
Lightning Source LLC
Chambersburg PA
CBHW071425160426
43195CB00013B/1814